WILDCATTERS

A Story of Texans, Oil, and Money

By Sally Helgesen

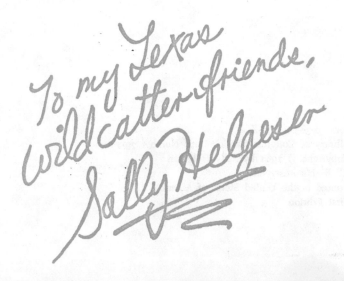

For my father, Charles Helgesen

My special thanks to a few people in Fort Worth,

Jane and John Graves
Olivia and Tony Bernabei
Jane and the late Rick Brown

ISBN: 0-385-14637-X
Library of Congress Catalog Card Number 79-7867
Copyright © 1981 by Sally Helgesen
All Rights Reserved
Printed in the United States of America
First Edition

Contents

Preface

PEOPLE often ask me how I came to write this book. Was I originally from Texas? Did I have friends in the oil business? Did I have a special interest, an expertise? What was the connection that made it possible for a young woman in her late twenties to gain access to the private workings of a world notorious for its clannishness?

The answer is that I had no connection, no expertise, no background. My mother's family had originally come from Texas, the German hill country around New Braunfels, but there were no longer any friends or relatives that I knew in the state who could help me out. I had in fact never been to Texas before I began working on this book. It was less a labor of love for me than an instrument of discovery.

I came to Dallas in the fall of 1977 with a few hundred dollars and a vague assignment from *Harper's Magazine* to write something about the state. I had wangled the assignment because I wanted to get out of New York for a while. I chose Dallas as my starting point because I'd heard the city was friendly and I guessed that I might be able to persuade some friendly soul to rent me a car despite the fact that I had no credit cards. Someone did.

The Cullen Davis murder trial was in progress in Amarillo, and I quickly decided that this should be my story. I stayed in Dallas for a week or so and spent a few evenings at the bar in the old Stoneleigh Hotel, where I learned the names of a few of Amarillo's leading families and heard background on the case. And then I drove north one morning to that old cattle town.

My lonely drive took me 400 miles along Route 287, past fabled half-million-acre ranches—the Waggoner, the Four Sixes—across the dry Red River bed with its groves of cottonwoods and pecan trees, through tiny towns where cotton balls blew through the streets like snow, and up finally (for this drive rises steadily 3,000 miles) to the high, bright cap rock that defines the high plains with its gulches, its mesas, and its table-like flatness. I had lately been seized by the gloomy belief that every place in America was becoming identical to every other place, but my drive proved dramatically the untenableness of this belief. And so my drive convinced me of the need to find some project that would give me reason to spend a year or so in Texas. I felt like I was chasing something across those wide and empty plains, and I knew it would take me some time to find it.

Someone at the Stoneleigh Bar had advised me to go see Stanley Marsh as soon as I arrived in Amarillo. Marsh, the heir to vast landholdings under which lie the world's largest helium reserves, is the local character, known for his sponsorship of such odd projects as the erection of a giant pool table atop an Amarillo office building and the planting of a "garden" of upended Cadillacs in a row along Helium Road. I visited Marsh the first morning after my arrival. He proved an affable, awkward, kindly-mannered giant who spoke in circumlocuities that made him difficult to understand. He offered to escort me to the Davis trial and introduce me around.

Davis was a Fort Worth millionaire, the heir to an oil drilling equipment fortune, who had been accused of killing his estranged wife's lover and her daughter and wounding two others in a midnight shooting spree at his six-million-dollar mansion. There had been a change of venue, and Davis was being tried in Amarillo. On the day I arrived in town, his wife Priscilla, a bleached blonde with huge siliconed breasts, had begun her testimony. She'd arrived at the courthouse wearing a cross around her neck, a phony schoolgirl dress, and carrying a Bible. She had outraged the sensibilities of the local townspeople: did she think they were such hicks as to believe her ridiculous act? Davis was being defended by Richard (Racehorse) Haynes, the silver-tongued Houston lawyer made famous by the "Blood and Money" case, and his presence made the trial a national cause célèbre.

Stanley Marsh introduced me to the local district attorney, then holding court with his witticisms in a small room at the courthouse. He welcomed me "aboard." In the evening, I hung out at Rhett Butler's, a tavern located under a highway access ramp on the way to an Amarillo suburb; the judge from the trial, the defense attorneys, and the many journalists covering the case took their refreshment there, and the atmosphere of camaraderie and relaxed enjoyment that unexpectedly characterized the courthouse pervaded Rhett Butler's as well. In this isolated backwater, under the wide black night, outsiders hung together.

I'd become interested in the trial because it seemed to offer a way of writing about one of the rather conventional themes that interested me then—the decline of the family, of general morality, of inherited responsibilities in modern American life. But a good look at the realities of this particular case disabused me of the notion of twisting it to fit the sense of malaise I myself was harboring at the time. Davis seemed simply the weak, spoiled, perverse second son of a clever but nasty little man known as "Stinky," whose reputation as a monster and conniver went unchallenged throughout the state. No decline in good old-fashioned values here; merely an evidence of the sense of purposelessness that so often comes in tandem with inherited riches. The trial, which I was attending faithfully, failed to interest me very much once I realized that it presented me with no theme, spoke of nothing larger than itself, was only about a tawdry crime of silly passions. The real story seemed to be in Amarillo.

Amarillo had its Taco Plazas and lonely shopping centers, those outcroppings of standardization that depressed me so much in the rest of America, but I thought that I could see through them to an older spirit that lay beneath. I had never visited a city of substantial size in which the almost shocking friendliness of the small town was so in evidence. "Glad you're visiting with us" was the constant refrain, and people invited me to share their guest rooms just because I was an outsider. In the evenings, I sometimes visited Stanley Marsh, the slightly wiggy philosopher-king, at his ranch-house, Toad Hall. It seemed, with its masses of brick and stone and open blazing fireplaces, like some medieval lord's manor house; a Volkswagen planted with its nose in the air stood like some twisted steel gorgon, always on guard at the end of the driveway. Stanley Marsh, sipping Bourbon and holding forth about life in his village, seemed very like a medieval lord.

I understood that Amarillo, made rich by Texas cattle shipped there to grow fat in feedlots before going north to slaughter, was undergoing a boom in the oil business at the time. And I understood that the oil business in Texas, like the cattle business, was very much a family enterprise, tied to the land and to inheritance. If these businesses were responsible for giving shape and substance to a town like Amarillo, I wanted to know about them.

Marsh took me to see his brother Tom, a wonderfully handsome young man who had spent time in other places but had come back home to Amarillo to run the family's oil interests. Tom Marsh told me what the independent oil business was, how it was booming now because of high prices, why it had been depressed for so many years by low ceilings, and how the younger generation of men like himself were coming back home to take advantage of the situation. He spoke of the business as operating along frontiers, and declared that the frontier spirit was still alive.

Tom Marsh introduced me to a variety of old wildcatters in Amarillo, men who'd been drilling some of the deepest wells on the American continent. I visited some of the ranches where they were drilling, vast empty tracts of scrub, flat and *sorry* (as the people there said), and I saw oil pumps punctuating the skyline. "Those are our mother cows," a rancher told me. "Without them, we couldn't afford to raise our beef."

I engaged in a few debates with wildcatters and other locals who insisted that there was some kind of conspiracy among the Eastern press to portray them and their business in a bad light. "They act like we're illegal," one man said. I answered that this was not so, although I knew very well that back in New York City, the simple description "Texas oilman" had unsavory connotations: saying a politician counted them among his friends was like saying that the suspect in a murder case had dated "a blond divorcée." It was difficult to reconcile this standard image with the old wildcatters I was meeting, men who talked so much about their independence and policies of plain dealing. I knew there was an established bias against some of the things I was seeing, and I began to want to help to correct that by writing objectively about them. The spirit that fired the men I was meeting seemed to be something that I was missing in America recently, and finding a renaissance of it made me feel more optimistic. The idea of a book took shape in my mind.

Tom Marsh introduced me to Max Banks, whom he said

was the smartest man he knew. Max Banks, a blustery, red-haired Irishman, was a panhandle rig contractor who did some wildcatting on the side; when I first entered his office he warned me with a shout: "Young lady, I'm tough. Tough as whang-leather." He said that I'd have to be tough to deal with him, and proved it later that afternoon by flying his twin-engine plane at odd angles while taking me on a tour of the Panhandle. Max Banks thought that I might be interested in writing about him for "the character angle," but he said he didn't mind how I played him up so long as I represented his business fairly. He wanted the people of America to "stop blaming oilmen every time two ducks died somewhere," to stop thinking that "just because a guy in Texas is making money he must be a crook or a son of a bitch," and so he felt it was his duty to let a writer from New York in on his business. I was to hear some version of these sentiments repeated by every oilman I would meet over the next fourteen months.

I spent nearly two weeks in the company of Max Banks, during which time I flew several times in his little plane to visit isolated oil patches spread out under magnificent skies and see his supply yards full of pipe and pumps. I watched him "make action" from the centralized "action room" in his big, elaborately modern office. I listened to him reflect mournfully about how he "might be out of date" because he still believed that the point of America was growth and development and enrichment of people and land. I saw him run a large and prosperous company with a personal style well suited to an earlier day. And I saw in Max Banks what I had seen in Amarillo all along, an unchangingness in the way things were done despite an appearance of modernness.

I drove south from Amarillo to Fort Worth because I'd heard people I met in Dallas talk of Fort Worth as *the* oil town to visit. I was given a long, hospitable, first-day tour of the town by an old oilman called "Pappy," whose son I had met during my stay in Dallas. Pappy, just returned from a week of planting pear and pecan trees on his ranch, drove me slowly through the west-side suburbs, pointing out granite villas, Spanish estates, turreted gingerbread fantasies, while giving me brief histories of the oil-rich families that inhabited them. He showed me the elaborate Tudor-style house behind the golf course where Cullen Davis had grown up, and he talked about how "bad blood" could be inherited. "Here in Texas, we've watched our bulls. We know you have to breed 'em right if you want to get good stock." He spoke proudly of all the good stock right here in Fort Worth, and he mentioned the Moncrief family as an example of "too much money gone *right*," as opposed to the Davis family, where money had gone wrong.

During the next nine months I spent in Fort Worth, I spent time with perhaps twenty-five oilmen there and in Dallas, Abilene, and Albany. I went to Amarillo again, and I visited well sites from far West Texas to Shreveport, Louisiana. I heard hundreds of stories of rags-to-riches and riches-to-even-greater-riches, but I always heard the same themes that Pappy and Max Banks and Tom Marsh had first sounded, repeated over and over: the new boom, and the new generation's part in it, the necessity for independence, the importance of family, of breeding, of stock. And always—in bars in Dallas and Fort Worth, in petroleum clubs, in offices and on rig sites—I heard about the fabulous, wealthy Moncrief family, "Old Monty," as he was always called, and his grandson "Dickie Bird" who was drilling up the Gulf of Suez. References to them always intrigued me, but the Moncriefs weren't the kind of people whom one just called and asked to visit. They'd had their share of personal tragedy, everyone said, and they were very, very private.

Several months afterward, when I was spending long hours with the Moncriefs, people in Texas would ask me how I ever got them to open their doors and their lives to a stranger, a journalist. Partly, it was just a matter of my having stayed around long enough, having established myself as a fixture on the scene, somebody who knew a lot of people and who therefore seemed trustworthy. And partly it was the desire that Monty Moncrief, like Max Banks, voiced time and again, to "see something objective written about all us down here for once." I was convinced, almost from the first time I heard about the family, that it would provide me with the best means for telling my story.

The famous clannishness of this stratum of Texas society makes it difficult for an outsider to gain access to the people who move within it. But once the outsider has gotten even the smallest bit inside, getting around becomes very easy because everyone knows everyone else and is glad to help. I found the people I met in Texas extraordinarily hospitable. During the fourteen months I spent in the state, I stayed only three weeks at a hotel; the rest of the time, I was the houseguest of different people whom I'd never met before, people with no direct relationship to the oil business who had nothing to gain from me. I was lent cars when my succession of $500 vehicles broke down, was given rides and introductions, and was asked to parties and cotillions. At times my lonely vigil in the state felt curiously like a triumphant tour, with parties and dinners given in my honor.

I had come to Texas with the intention of writing something pessimistic about how families were falling apart, how everything in American life was changing. But my purposes revealed more about my own state of mind than anything else, and what I actually found and stayed to write was a story about families that stayed together and a way of life that exhibited a surprising continuity. My experiences in Texas changed me into an optimist in regard to the American free enterprise system, and filled me with hope for the future of this country. I became convinced also that the entrenchment of large bureaucracies will mean the death of whatever measure of frontier spirit still exists.

SALLY HELGESEN,
New York, 1980

1

Better Luck Next Time

IT WAS October 31, 1978, Halloween. The day was bright
and hot in Fort Worth, Texas, not bad for a game of golf,
but it was a little late for that now. The Rivercrest Country
Club was closing its course. The sun was still high, but already ghosts and goblins were crisscrossing the putting
greens, carrying paper sacks as they flitted between the gray
Tudor castles and pink granite villas that encircled the
club's well-watered green.

Dick Moncrief was not considering a game of golf today,
however. Nor were his thoughts with those of others in this
tradition-minded part of the world, where daddies fly in
from across half a continent to take a child trick-or-treating.
No, Dick Moncrief—scion, grandson, and heir to one of the
great oil families in Texas—had other things on his mind as
the late autumn dusk began to settle. It looked as if some
ghosts and goblins of his own were about to come knocking
at the door today.

On the other side of the globe, drill ships floated in the
old unquiet waters of the Gulf of Suez. From upon these

ships and the platforms around them, Louisiana Cajuns and Bedouin tribesmen displaced by war and changing times probed deep into the rock that underlay the sea. The rock was rich: it yielded 40,000 barrels of oil each day. The oil was lined directly into the hulls of Greek transport tankers waiting nearby, and hauled off discreetly to the Israeli mainland. And although the world had not been aware of it until the autumn of 1978, this particular Middle Eastern oil province was claimed not by any Arab nation, but by the state of Israel.

But the Israelis had not discovered the province, nor were they producing its oil. Texas wildcatters had done those jobs, getting by on grit and intuition, as Texas wildcatters always do. The "Israeli Deal," as it was being called back home in Fort Worth, had been executed by Dick Moncrief, and the friends he had brought in on this great and secret oil business deal.

They had struck oil in the Suez Gulf the year before, in November of 1977. Their strike had been a real wildcatter's dream, for oil ran through a succession of rock horizons in the field, one rich vein underlying another. But these hidden depths were of little comfort to Dick Moncrief now, for it looked as if Israel was going to return the area to Egypt, which continued to claim possession. Dick Moncrief had become accustomed to proclaiming that his discovery in Israel was "the greatest deal in the world," but by the autumn of 1978, the greatest deal was disappearing into a devil's spout of turbulence and confusion, unpredictable and deadly as a sandstorm in the desert.

Dick Moncrief's group, a secret Texas consortium by the name of Western Desert, had been granted exclusive mineral rights to the Gulf of Suez and a stretch of Sinai desert in the north by the Israeli government. But Israel only occupied the land, which it had won from Egypt in the 1967 war between those two countries. Now, eleven years after the war and only one year since the territory had proven its real worth, it appeared that Israel would suddenly be giving it back to Egypt.

Dick Moncrief had always known that this might happen one day, but he'd chosen to gamble that it would take a long time, as things in the Middle East usually did. In the last few months, however, the American government had begun pressing for an immediate resolution, a quick peace. The Egyptian President, Anwar Sadat, was meeting with the Israeli Prime Minister, Menachem Begin, at Blair House on Pennsylvania Avenue to negotiate the terms of their settlement. Dick Moncrief, sitting helplessly by in Fort Worth, wondered what he might do to redeem his name, his reputation, and the forty million dollars his investors had risked, should the greatest deal in the world be lost to him.

So it was that he suddenly found himself at the very apex of history. Nevertheless, in time-honored oil business fashion, he had contrived to stay well behind the scenes. The New York *Times* had run some enthusiastic stories about Israel's big oil strikes, but they contained no hint as to who was behind the discoveries. And *Business Week* had revealed that "some Americans" were behind the sudden blooming of Israel's newest and most secret resource, but the magazine had not mentioned names. Dick Moncrief had courted anonymity throughout the thirty-five years of his life, and even during the course of this wild and highly visible deal, he'd managed to remain in the shadows.

Shadows, indeed, crowded in upon Dick Moncrief. One, long and deadly, was cast by a major oil company that sought to take away all he had worked for when the peace which threatened his peace was proclaimed. Amoco, one of the "Seven Sisters" of the international oil business, had been granted a production-sharing contract to the Gulf of Suez by Egypt before the 1967 war, and the company very naturally contested Dick Moncrief's right to be there. Letters of warning and threats of suit arrived in Fort Worth regularly, and now that the American government was

pressing the terms of peace, Dick Moncrief doubted that his
cause would find favor over that of Amoco, for major companies exerted a lobbying power in Washington that no independent could hope to match. What was it Richard Nixon
had told Dick Moncrief's grandfather Monty when the older
man had flown to Washington with a group from Fort
Worth to plead the independent's cause? "There's just not
enough of you boys, that's the trouble," the President had
said. "You'll never get any support in Washington on that
account." At least Nixon had been honest about it, Monty
Moncrief said. But the shadow that loomed behind Amoco's
was more vivid and frightening in its way, for it was the
shadow by which Dick Moncrief measured himself. It was
cast by W. A. Moncrief—Monty, as he was always called—
grandfather and patriarch of the Fort Worth oil clan.

Monty Moncrief was one of Texas's great wildcatting legends, and it was of course because of him that Dick Moncrief had gotten himself into the Israeli Deal in the first.
place. Not that his grandfather had ever supported or encouraged him in what the older man considered a foolish endeavor—not at all. But his grandfather's shadow was such a
powerful one that Dick Moncrief knew from the very beginning that he would have to do something wild and daring if
he hoped to become anything more than simply Monty
Moncrief's grandson. "Granddad did it all in America," he
said when asked why he went into Israel. "There was nothing left for me to do here."

Rumor in Texas has made the story of Dick Moncrief's
first confrontation with his grandfather over Israel into a
legend of classic simplicity: as legend, it is a refined and per-
fected version of the truth. The meeting is said to have occurred in the early 1970s, on the golf course at the Rivercrest Country Club on the west side of Fort Worth. Upon
this unassuming stretch of sod uncounted million-dollar
deals have been struck; no small part of America's economic
history might be traced along its green, well-tended length.

Monty Moncrief, at the time of the story, was deep into his seventies, and regularly shooting his age. He was approached by his grandson, then hardly in his thirties, who had begun to fancy himself heir apparent to his grandfather. The conceit surprised a lot of people in town, who considered him something of a dilettante, the third generation descendant of a legend, a kid with water instead of blood in his veins.

The young man talked of many things before he finally came around to the point. It was his conviction that there was oil to be found in the lands Israel had seized from Egypt in 1967. The land was occupied now, subject to dispute, but Dick Moncrief believed that the Israelis, desperate for every ounce of petroleum they could lay hold of, might nevertheless be willing to grant an outsider drilling rights on the territory until such time as it might be lost again by war or by treaty.

A private oil business family would have to make the deal, of course. No big company would dare provoke Arab wrath and thereby risk its other investments. Besides, big companies worked clumsily, like dinosaurs, encumbered by the need to pass decisions through a maze of channels, and this deal demanded lightning speed and absolute secrecy. Only an independent could bring it off, the young man believed, and he saw no reason why the Moncriefs, who ranked unsurpassed in the hierarchy of Texas oil, should not be the family to do it.

The older man said nothing in response to his grandson's proposal. He lined up slowly for his next shot. He selected his wood and drove straight down the fairway, sending his ball impossibly far. Then he looked at his grandson.

"B.L.N.T.," he said—*better luck next time.* And he turned on his heel and walked after his ball.

Rumor in Texas has repeated this story, time after time. Its twist comes in its conclusion, *Red River* style. For Dick Moncrief confounded everyone in town and decided to

pursue the Israeli Deal all by himself, just as the young
cattleman in that famous Western story drove the herd
northward when his adoptive father turned back on the trail
to Abilene. Dick Moncrief pursued the deal despite his
grandfather's refusal to join him, pursued it despite the opposition of his own father, Tex, as well. He pursued it because it seemed to him that just as fate had bestowed upon
him the blessing of having been born a Moncrief, so had it
also thrust on him the burden of challenging the man who
made being a Moncrief worthy of particular note. And he
stuck with his decision even though at times (as now, on
Halloween, more than five years later) it seemed that it
might in truth be *better luck never* for him.

"I guess I've been beaten down," he told a visitor from a
world far away as he sat at his desk that autumn evening.
But of course he had not been, and his story still had a long
way to go.

Dick Moncrief's story, and that of the grandfather who
preceded him and so made possible everything that followed, is typical of thousands of Texas stories, though perhaps more spectacular in its details; the stakes Dick Moncrief plays for are always higher because the ante was
upped by the man who started it all. And yet it is the like-
ness of his story to so many others in Texas that gives it a
real and transcendent importance. For it reveals in a human
way what is happening in the American oil business today,
beyond the abstractions of Wall Street trading sheets.

People will tell you that Texas is different, and then they
will undertake to define that difference. It is bigger, they
will say—that's obvious. It is richer, they will say—that's obvious too. Texas is unashamed, Texas is boastful, Texas is everything every other place is, only more so. These things are
true, of course, but although they explain why Texas is special, they do not explain why it is different.

What makes Texas different is not so much its money as its blood, and its awareness of that blood. It is not the blood spilled in Saturday night brawls or shed in the bizarre murders whose trials make headlines around the country, but rather the blood of human bloodlines. In Texas, there is always an awareness—a cattlebreeder's awareness, it might be, or a stockman's—of exactly whose blood runs through a man's or a woman's veins, and of what that blood demands. People in Texas are raised to be what others in their families have been, or at least they are in those two most Texan of family businesses, oil and cattle. Family is destiny here, as surely as it is within the *cosce* of the Mafia. Success is measured by what one achieves beyond what those who went before achieved.

In America, in the 1970s, it was not universally assumed that a young man would feel a responsibility to do whatever his grandfather and father had done, or feel the need to surpass them in order to prove himself worthy of their blood. The story of right succession and inheritance is the oldest story in the world, but it is no longer always a familiar one in a world entirely changed, a world in which families break up, sons do not routinely follow their fathers, and the wealth of the land that binds people together is no longer so easily come by or kept. And yet it is a story that may still be told in Texas, where the old truths are held to be self-evident. Here, the young bulls still lock horns with the old bulls and fight to inherit the earth. And that's what makes Texas different.

Dick Moncrief might have confounded the expectations of those in Fort Worth who never imagined that he would break away and do something bold on his own. He might have confounded those from outside such a town who assume that the mantle of succession no longer falls heavily upon those of the younger generation who inherit it. But by presenting his grandfather with a challenge he could refuse that day (so legend has it) in the early 1970s on the Rivercrest Country Club golf course, Dick Moncrief was simply showing his blood, doing what he had been bred up to do. Opportunity lay open before him and he was inspired to walk in the footsteps of a giant.

2

The Wild Cutting Edge
of the Frontier

THE OLD BULLS in this story—the giants, the men of Monty Moncrief's generation—came into the oil business in the wild old days of the open frontier. Everywhere they looked, they saw opportunity without limits. The land itself was empty, and so these men built cities upon it and founded dynasties. They left behind them a world made in their own image. They gave shape to a business and to a way of life, and their deeds made them legends.

The major oil companies, which would one day almost destroy the independents, had not yet consolidated their power. Those companies were still independents themselves. Exxon, as one old Dallas wildcatter remembers it, "was just the Humble then, a fly-by-night Burkburnett outfit"; Burkburnett, a North Texas boomtown named for a million-acre cattle baron, was more significant than the scrappy little company. Nor had the iron hand of Rockefeller's Standard Oil empire yet consolidated its grip. In time, it would seize control of the flow of oil by monopolizing its distribution. Writing of the Seven Sisters, Anthony Sampson characterizes Texas as "the wild cutting edge of the industry," and in the old days, those wild-edge conditions prevailed everywhere.

The business then was open to any white man who could hustle up the money for a rig, talk a farmer into leasing the mineral rights to his land, and then maintain enough optimism or pigheadedness to drill up his leasehold until he either found oil or convinced himself that he had made a mistake. If he was successful, he reinvested his profits and bought new leases; if enough of his wells came through, he became a genuine oilman and founded a dynasty of his own. If he failed to find oil, he either abandoned the entire enterprise, or hustled up some more money and tried again. It was that simple.

As frontiersmen, the old wildcatters had neither the time nor the inclination to question their own purposes, or to agonize about what the future consequences of their efforts might be. They just went out and did whatever was there to be done, filling in the blank spaces across an empty horizon. And so they appeared, to those come of age in a more cautious era, to be true American heroes, the very stuff of legend, and perhaps above all, *real men*. Circumstances made for opportunity, and opportunity, they say, makes the man.

But circumstances in the oil business began to change drastically after the Second World War. In 1954, the Supreme Court ruled in a case brought against Phillips Petroleum that the Federal Power Commission had the authority to set the price for natural gas shipped between the states. The commission then set the price at seventeen cents for each thousand cubic feet, and there it stayed for many a long dry year.

The oil business in the United States had been dependent upon the sale of natural gas, which is often produced as a by-product when oil is drilled; gas, which is lighter and

more refined, gives oil its buoyancy, and it flows naturally
when pressure on the rock reservoir is relieved. Therefore,
when a price ceiling was set on gas, the entire petroleum
business fell into immediate decline. Drilling costs increased
rapidly over the next few decades, both because of inflation
and because new sources of gas had to be sought in deeper
strata as old wells emptied the shallower deposits. A
5,000-foot well, for example, sunk in the early 1950s, might
have cost a wildcatter twenty thousand dollars to drill,
while twenty years later, gas was being produced from
30,000 feet underground, and wells routinely cost three-
quarters of a million dollars. The economics got worse with
each passing year, and soon the search for gas in America
ceased entirely.

Meanwhile, the low price set for natural gas was developing a wasteful appetite for this particularly clean fuel. When
the domestic supply began to run out because no new wells
were being drilled in America, this appetite was satisfied by
importing Algerian gas and synthetics produced in the Middle East. There were no price ceilings imposed upon these
foreign products, so soon Americans were paying producers
abroad four times as much as they could pay for gas found
in their own country.

During the years that price limits were discouraging the
search for natural gas, the search for oil in America was
being discouraged for different reasons but to the same
effect. Before the Second World War, the major oil companies had begun acquiring concessions to drill for oil
abroad. A few wildcatters had blazed the way, most notably
in Mexico, where a Yorkshire contractor had gained title to
virtually all the oil in that country at the beginning of the
century. Exxon and Mobil then established themselves in
Iraq, Socal and Texaco took concessions to the sands of
Arabia, Gulf appropriated Kuwait, and the Seven Sisters
divided among them the riches of Iran.

It was easier and cheaper for multi-national companies

with lots of cash to buy concessions in what has since become known as the Third World than to acquire mineral
rights at home. America is the only country in the world in
which such rights are privately owned; everywhere else, except in a small area of Saskatchewan, the state or crown
holds title. And so in America, mineral rights must be purchased from thousands of individual landowners. The big
companies very naturally preferred to make their deals with
a single sheik or tyrant for the wealth of an entire nation instead of dickering with countless farmers in order to put together a field. By the early 1950s, then, the majors were
flooding America with oil from abroad. It was cheap, and it
looked like it would be cheap for a long time.

Thus it was that the independents began to take over the
domestic oil business, while the majors abandoned it. The
wildcatters' competitive, individual way of working was
compatible with the private ownership of the land. But the
independents could not compete against the low prices of oil
being brought in from abroad, and the economics of their
business continued to get worse.

Favorable import quotas helped the majors establish
themselves in the Middle East. Because the government
permitted them to count foreign royalty payments as taxes
paid abroad, the big companies could keep the price of imported oil low and so destroy the market for the domestic
product. Such policies, directly beneficial to the big oil im-
porters, were a reflection of the major companies' lobbying
power in Washington. Conversely, the price ceilings and increasing welter of legal prohibitions and regulations that
began to choke domestic production after the early '50s
were evidence of the independents' weakness in Washington. Government policies encouraged importing oil instead
of producing it in America.

In the early 1950s, independent oil producers began to
warn that America would soon find herself ransomed to the
oil-producing nations if she continued to rely upon imported

oil. But they found that their warnings were regarded as suspicious by reason of self-interest and assumed to be rooted in a hopelessly outdated xenophobia as well. It seemed inconceivable then that the underdeveloped countries of the world would ever conspire to threaten American power. And so the independents languished, while the majors waxed fat, importing oil from abroad.

In the early 1950s, there had been 10,000 independent oilmen in America; twenty years later, there were scarcely more than 2,000. It looked as if the independent was being driven into extinction, like the range-riding cowboy before him. "We were but creatures of circumstances, the circumstance of the unfenced world," the anonymous cowboy had sung after the invention of barbed wire brought the enfencement of the wide-open plain. Now the fences of control and restriction and the barriers of foreign competition were changing circumstance for the wildcatter, that inheritor of the cowboy's nomadic tradition. The frontier was closing, and the frontiersmen were disappearing as it did. Limited opportunity began to shape a very different kind of man.

The second generation in Texas oil inherited the huge wealth gained by their parents' ceaseless activity. But the business in which the money had been made had gone bad, and the inheritors were left with little to do except preserve what had already been won and spend whatever they wished. Plowing their fortunes back into the earth would have proved of little profit in the decades that followed World War II, and so the sons of the original wildcatters rarely tried to extend their fathers' discoveries. The young bulls of the middle generation found no terrain on which they might challenge the old bulls' achievements. Their mood became one of defensiveness and retreat.

"The men of my father's era spent all their time sitting on their duffs playing poker at the local petroleum club or just watching their real estate appreciate," a third-generation oilman from Amarillo named Tom Marsh once said. "But my generation is like my grandfather's," he added. "We're *not content.*"

Tom Marsh's maxim may be taken as a general rule, defining the split between the second and third generations in the Texas oil business. Grandsons here have taken as their heroes the old wildcatters who founded the family businesses. And so they are injecting something of the old-time, pioneering spirit into a business gone decadent or diverse.

This has not occurred because of any leapfrogging of biology or instinct, however. It has rather happened because the frontier began opening up again in the early 1970s, just as the younger generation was coming of age.

In the autumn of 1973, the newly formed alliance of oil-rich nations that called itself OPEC met for the first time in Vienna. There, to the surprise of the world, the cartel asserted its power and independence. The OPEC alliance began immediately to raise its prices for oil higher each year, and then higher each several months. The major companies, which would benefit greatly from this strategy, were nevertheless thrown into confusion by it. They began to lose much of their power—the power, for example, to set prices—as their independence and identity was subsumed by governments that formerly had been nothing but clients.

This surprising turn of events inadvertently altered the disastrous circumstances in which American independents had found themselves for the last twenty years. Policymakers in Washington began to realize that a domestic oil business depressed by price ceilings and rendered unable to compete against imports had worked against every possible American interest. Price ceilings on gas were permitted to rise slowly during the next few years, and a series of controls placed upon oil by Richard Nixon in a foolish and untimely attempt to stop inflation were gradually removed.

The rise was relative, of course. Domestic producers still had to sell their product at lower prices than those which

Middle Eastern nations could ask. And the increasing number of bureaucratic considerations, governing everything from the distance of a well from an old Indian burial ground to the number of portable toilets that must surround an isolated rig-site, continued to increase as governmental agencies proliferated. And yet the change in price structure was enough to encourage exploration once more. It began slowly at first, and then assumed boom proportions. As a consequence of the first OPEC meeting, the independents came back into the fields once again.

Or rather their grandsons did. Responding to the circumstances of the new frontier, many among the third generation took their own measure against that of the men who had first cast their shadows upon the empty land. And so Dick Moncrief was not unusual in challenging his grandfather's achievement. He was simply making a dramatic bid to succeed him, and choosing the scale that would suit Monty Moncrief's particular stature. The same thing was happening all over Texas.

3

Of Grandfathers and Heroes

THE CHANGE in frontier circumstance worked neatly with time-honored Texas tradition, for grandfather-heroes are a common breed here. Family pantheons are animated with the spirits of forebears in this part of the country, where tales of ancestral daring and true grit are part of the larger frontier legend.

This is partly because history lies close to the surface in the recently settled West, and one's own grandfather has often given direct and discernible shape to the land. It is partly because—the weather being warm, and the pull of a harsh land won at great cost being especially strong—grandparents in Texas rarely abandon the towns where they have raised their families and venture forth to "senior citizen" ghettos in Florida or Arizona. They live where they have always lived, and their daily presence keeps their legends alive. And it is also because young people here rarely leave the old hometown for good. All over the state, one meets young men and women of great wealth who could live anywhere, who indeed have lived for a time in New York or Paris or Los Angeles or London, but who have come back to Amarillo or Abilene and done whatever they were bred up to do. Those who have inherited what their families so recently claimed take their birthright seriously.

And finally, the mystique of grandfather-heroes exists partly because grandfathers play a special, in-between role in this land of men impossibly hard and women improbably soft, for often it seems as if fathers can show their kinder natures only when the challenge a younger man presents is one generation removed. One recalls the familiar image of Lyndon Johnson listening to tales of the Wild West on his grandfather's knee, while waiting in vain for a kind word from his father. All over Texas the story is the same. "My daddy was a tough old bull, but when he told me it was time to quit law school and come to work for him, I did it, even though it was the hardest thing in the world for me, and even though he told me I'd have to run him out of business before I could get my share," explained Larry Meeker, a smaller-stakes oilman who grew up not far from the Moncriefs. But when he speaks of his grandfather, who started the family business, who tore his own sons from their work as carpenters in the Panhandle and herded them down to the West Texas boom, Larry Meeker lets the tears roll down his cheeks, and he is not ashamed. He recalls the old man's flinty kindness, and he is proud to have withstood the assaults of his father's pride so that he might take his place among his grandfather's descendants.

Traveling through oil country, one becomes aware of a similarity among all the tales told of grandfathers who first subdued the land and claimed its riches. Like mythic heroes, the men of the first generation begin to seem interchangeable after a while, like figures cut from the same rough magnificent fabric—uncured cowhide perhaps. The stories repeated about them—stories of wild nights, huge strikes, lucky breaks, desperate losses, stories of families that disappointed them in big ways but which finally carried on in true dynastic spirit—are meant to give instances of their prickly individuality, but all the stories seem to be about the same prickly individual. The older men's utterances, intended to show them as colorful, show them in all the same colors. Each stands invested with an aura akin to that of every other among them; each is strong, agile, bold and clever, plain-spoken, without guile, and always proud. They are giants, like Davy Crockett, successful predators, acute and astute, tamers of the untamable and defenders of vast treasure. They are the very essence of legend, predictable yet real. And the similarities among them do not make these heroes any less real, for many among them have been carved on a large scale indeed.

In the autumn of 1978, the season during which the Middle East peace talks in Washington were claiming his grandson's attentions, Monty Moncrief was eighty-four years old. He was still very much the patriarch of his clan, the man who made the decisions in his family and in his family's business. Family and business were in fact the same thing with him, the desire to found the one being inseparably tied to the desire to found the other. When speaking of his business, he never mentioned himself specifically. *We went there*, he would always say, *we signed the deal, we figured it was best.* "This is a *we* kind of business," he explained when asked about it. "We don't tolerate any of that *I* stuff around here." In Texas, in the oil business, one sees as nowhere else that the ideal of capitalism is the ideal of founding a family and conferring the right of inheritance upon it, passing a legacy on.

"We're oilmen," Monty Moncrief would answer, when asked about ranching, about real estate, about whether he flew his own plane. "We're oilmen" meant that anything which extended beyond the realm of oil was not a proper Moncrief concern. "We're one-hundred percent family owned, unincorporated, and independent, and we intend to stay that way," he liked to say. And his grandson, reflecting upon the complexities of doing business abroad, would explain that if he himself really wanted to do things right, he'd set up a big public company and go after what he wanted. "Except that's not the way my family does things," he added, eliminating the idea as a matter of course. In the shadow world of oil promoters, one sometimes meets with independents who have bought and sold their way through six or seven businesses, who indeed start those businesses with the aim of going public and selling out as soon as possible. To Monty Moncrief, such a strategy is unimaginable. Moncrief Oil is synonymous with himself, his dynasty. Continuity is what his blood demands.

He was, at the age of eighty-four, as big and as strong as a bull. His bearing—commanding, imperial, yet always in calm repose—put one in mind of a dragon as well, curious yet guarding his cave with complete assurance. He possessed the directness and the utter simplicity of the old and the truly great. When he met people from outside his world, he got a fix on them by asking such things as where they grew up, the number of children in their family, how their parents had met. It was by knowing the kitchen-table side of their lives that he judged whom he might trust. The folksiness of his method belied its wiliness.

He was every bit the picture of the oil patriarch, handsome and sharp-eyed and deep-voiced and tall, and he had those long earlobes strangely characteristic of the titans of Texas. He walked without a stoop, and he carried his large frame without a trace of fat; he had thick white hair and spectacles over which he gazed with the canniness of an old cardsharp. And indeed he seemed, with his agility, his courtly manners, and the anachronistic perfection of his tailoring—sky-blue trousers, two-toned Palm Springs shoes, dis-

creetly monogrammed shirts, and gay, well-brushed hats—to
be impervious to age, or to changing times.

His unquestioning confidence in the worthiness of his enterprise made him seem impervious as well to the doubts
and the questions about motives and meanings that inevitably beset later generations. Like others who first conquered
the open frontier and harnessed its resources for human use,
he kept his faith in the absolute value of building, of progress, of getting things done. When he spoke of his belief in
the enterprise of producing oil in America, one could almost
forget that he had made hundreds of millions of dollars
doing so. Such benefits sounded almost incidental to the
task of settling the land and mining its resources.

Perhaps this confidence is what set free the huge energies
of this first generation of giants. At the age of eighty-four,
this aging patriarch came into his office each morning at
eight and stayed there all day, unless the weather was particularly fine. In that event, he went to the Rivercrest Country Club and played nine holes of golf, or eighteen. He usually shot a score under his age. He was up early on
weekends for golf tournaments and hunting expeditions, on
which the number of birds he bagged inevitably became the
general topic of wonder. On Sundays, he was at church before anyone else was up. He traveled to Houston and to
Washington regularly in his own jet, and drove his cream-
colored Cadillac to work and around town himself. When
met by limousine at an airport, he conversed about the
countryside with the driver, while the men around him kept
their noses in their ledgers. The size of his spirit put him immediately at ease with those whom the more anxious or pre-
occupied might have ignored.

The woman to whom he had been married for sixty years
was not one to be outshone by all this masculine splendor.
She unleashed furious energies in the realm she claimed as
her own, tending whole greenhouses full of gardenias and
camelias, cranking up twenty quarts of ice cream at a time

for her children's families, rising early to bake more pies and cakes than any household could possibly consume, filling the houses of her husband's employees with an abundance of her own handiwork. Her house suffered a surfeit of such things by reason of enthusiasm. She drove herself around town in her own cream-colored Seville, which bore, in true Texas fashion, a license plate with her name on it, Liz.

Despite such natural touches of flamboyance, the old couple clung to the ways they had been raised to believe were right. They spurned, for example, the institutional art patronage that has become a way of life among the oil-rich of Texas. They contributed their millions privately, without benefit of foundations, to hospitals instead, explaining that their first duty was to alleviate human suffering. They extended themselves to such neglected gestures as bringing the extra food from a family party around to the local orphanage, a bit of old-fashioned thoughtfulness that touched their granddaughter-in-law Marsland, Dick Moncrief's wife, and caused her to reflect upon the less abstract humanity of the generation that was passing away.

The stories told about Monty Moncrief all reveal him as tough, canny, given to understatement, a man of action who wastes few words but can, when he wishes, move mountains —a typical Western hero, in short. The tale of his rejecting Dick Moncrief's challenge to go abroad—the smooth *B.L.N.T.* murmured as he made the perfect fairway drive—is just what one expects from this tradition. Another grandson, Charlie Moncrief, delights in stories about his grandfather's toughness. "Once my dad was bawling me out for something," he recalls, "and I was scared, but I talked back anyway. Granddad was reading the newspaper nearby. When my dad got done with me, Granddad turned, and without ever looking up he said, 'If that was my boy, I'd take him out and whomp his head against the cement.'" The story is told with glee, an echo of wonder can be discerned: *was ever a man so tough?* Of course Charlie, being Monty Mon-

crief's grandson, never had to endure the full measure of the
older man's toughness. His own father had to suffer that,
while the grandson is left free to admire it. Such is the pattern with grandfather-heroes in the West.

Like so many of the first generation who made their fortunes in oil, Monty Moncrief has never lived in anything
approaching splendor, but rather remains in the solid, simple, suburban comfort of the first home he ever built. Old
wildcatters' attitudes seem to be much like those of the original cattlemen, who preferred their familiar ranch home-
steads to the palatial quarters that their heirs built in town.
"My dad says he wants to live where he can eat his breakfast biscuits with German rice farmers in roadside slop-
houses," explained the very young son of a very old oilman
down in Houston, and variations upon this theme prevail
generally among the first generation.

The neighborhoods where the oil-rich of Fort Worth live
describe an arc to the west of the city, which maps like a
blueprint the changing styles of each succeeding generation.
The old neighborhood, dense with matured magnolias,
sweeps along the southern edge of the Rivercrest Country
Club golf course, and the homes that line it are large but no
more than comfortable; most of them, like Monty Moncrief's, are built in a vaguely English style, dark brick or
half-timbered. The style is perhaps absurd upon the bright
wind-washed river rise here where the live oak grows, but it
is a style that gives evidence of an allegiance to the Puritan
idea of tradition held sacred by the men who subdued the
harsh land and raised tree-shaded outposts upon the plains.
The allegiance is to pleasures neither luxurious nor sweet,
but to comforts won by sweat and handed down with an un-
derstanding of the duties entailed upon them.

The second generation, settling along the curve of the
river bend that stretches west from the Rivercrest, came of
age after the frontier had been settled. Not being driven by
the pioneering spirit of those who had gone before, they

abandoned the grave Anglophile style that spoke of duty and tradition and built for themselves wild rococo villas, Venetian palaces of gray granite, antebellum plantation estates, and gay, pink, gingerbread turreted fantasies. They tried, in styles that changed with every year, to evoke a suggestion of beauty and culture and luxury, rather than to make reference to a perceived sense of continuity. The display of wild eclecticism and chaotic individualism that wends westward from the Rivercrest gives evidence of a robber-baron mode of thought that ransacks not simply the treasures but the styles of disparate civilizations as well, and shows them forth as spoils. All traces of the frontier ideal have vanished from this cluttered preserve of received ideas, and only the hard brightness of the sun and the wide sky above remind one that this is the frontier West, the land of oil and cattle.

The Crestline neighborhood slopes gently down toward the more sober grid of Westover Hills, where the third generation lives. Some of the homes here reflect a softening of second generation taste, a liking for luxury that gives little to ostentation and so achieves a more harmonious style. Others are survivors of pure second-generation sensibility, crowded incongruously upon the new and more discreet scale. Among these must be counted the pink stone Roman temple, rising strangely amid a stand of oak scrub, which for years now has been in the process of being built by a high-spirited young oilman named Kelly Young and his wife, Connie, who comes very new to her wealth. "Our mistake here in town," commented the heiress to an old oil fortune, "was in taking poor Connie to New Orleans and letting her see all those columns."

Such fantasies are the exception, however. For extravagant though Westover Hills may be in terms of what homes there cost (six-million-dollar-prices are not unknown), it nevertheless echoes the sterner ethic of the old first-generation Rivercrest neighborhood, if not the self-restraint. The houses here reflect the spirit of dutifulness that has taken root among those for whom new frontiers lie open, however temporarily. Many have been built in the latest uniform style, buildings of pinkish-brown brick with windowless facades and low brick or stone enclosing walls which make them resemble nothing so much as suburban doctors' or dentists' offices, places of business that allude to responsibility. The homes here crest bare rolling hills that stand starkly against the harsh sunlight, hills flown over grimly all day long by the great black-bottomed B-52s that make incessant sorties from the Carswell Air Force Base directly to the north. Along this illustrative arc, the Moncrief family homes are obligingly spaced in accord with the prevailing generational scheme.

The three-story white stone and black glass Moncrief Building in downtown Fort Worth was built by Monty Moncrief's son Tex, whose office there adjoins his father's. Monty Moncrief describes this venture into real estate, a typically second-generation effort at diversification, as entirely his son's idea. The building is impressive in a modern, anonymous way, all glass and sleekness, its reception room hung with paintings of wildlife and strewn with copies of the *Oil and Gas Journal*. But here, as in the lobbies of bank towers down the street, where old wildcatters can be seen lounging about and exchanging information on wells, it doesn't take long to see through the modern facade to the unchanging reality of the way things are done in Texas.

A row of family Cadillacs stands slotted in a shaded spot alongside the building like horses at the tether. The visitor parks, enters, and is ushered without ceremony into Monty Moncrief's office. He is on the telephone, agreeing to drill a well for a family friend who has won an oil lease in the federal lottery and hopes to gain an annuity by it. The room is heavy with leather and slick with convenience, in the updated cattleman's style. Hung upon the walls are the inscribed photographs of Presidents and the mementos of official favor and recognition—honorary hard hats, sentimental citations—to which the men who fought in the two world wars ascribe a value ignored by a newer generation, which often dismisses them as hollow tokens, mere scraps of paper with no more than a literal value.

Monty Moncrief begins his discussion with politics. Like so many Texas oilmen, always eager to distinguish for the outsider how his world of handshake agreements and deals made on trust differs from the devious ways of the outside world, he speaks ruefully of such evil as he has found. He points to a picture of Richard Nixon, smiling down from the wall. Although the most luxurious of the Moncrief family planes—the BAC-111, as big as a DC-9—is put at the disposal of the former President whenever he travels south, Monty Moncrief is quick to tell the visitor that Nixon was "a weak man, destroyed by his own avarice." Lyndon Johnson's photograph is also very much in evidence, and Monty Moncrief, who knew him for many years, speaks of him as "a compassionate man, but greedy like Nixon, and much prouder than he."

Such judgments are not political, but personal. They are moral sentences passed upon men who were not large enough to live up to their offices, but to whom a measure of respect is nonetheless owed simply because they won and held those offices. If the first generation of frontier settlers were cut from the mold of heroes, they have also kept their faith in heroes, and they honor even those who have disgraced themselves. They exhibit personal pantheons across which fall the shadows of men who shaped America's destiny, as they themselves have shaped it in more anonymous ways.

4

No Guts, No Blue Chips

LIKE SO MANY first generation wildcatters, Monty Moncrief came to Texas by way of Oklahoma's rolling prairies. That state had been settled by an aggressive breed, the Sooners. They were the men who got there *sooner*, who chased the Indians from their bright red-hued land when it was thrown open for white settlement in 1889. They set their cattle to graze, bred horses, planted corn, built railroads and towns, and they drilled for oil. Then, they often moved on to Texas, or saw their sons move on. Opportunity looked larger there.

Monty Moncrief was born in Sulphur Springs, East Texas, but his family moved shortly afterward to Checotah, Oklahoma. His father had come as a child to Sulphur Springs in a covered wagon from Georgia after that state's devastation at the hands of Sherman. Most of the first settlers in the border region where East Texas, Eastern Oklahoma, and Southern Arkansas converge came there to escape Reconstruction, and their great-numbered migration has given to the region its particular Southern character.

The Southern cast of mind paid honor to a code of chivalry. Handshake agreements were the ideal, and a man's word was considered to be his bond. Such virtues were held to be in contrast with the legalistic ways of Yankee entrepreneurs, who were imagined to be more concerned with the letter than the spirit of the law. But such virtues were of course in even greater contrast with the traditional ways of this backwoods frontier region, where men and women on the wrong side of the law have always come to cool their heels in remote and unquestioning towns. This is a part of the country where (as a Texarkana man explained to a visitor) you never ask a stranger his name because he just might not want you to know what it is. The juxtaposition of Southern idealism and scrubland brutality that took root in this corner of the world created a strange hybrid, a people at once suspicious and warm, cunning and kind, sharp-trading and hospitable.

Monty Moncrief's family moved to Checotah when the town was still in Indian Territory. Like many another man, his father came there chasing the railroad that was everywhere blazing a trail across the empty spaces. He was a hardware merchant by trade, and he hoped to start a business that would profit from the boom that inevitably attended the opening of a new rail line. But like many another who gambled on the frontier, Monty Moncrief's father outwitted himself. For no sooner had he settled in Checotah than that "Katy" Railroad Company decided to veer its new course through Muskogee instead. Checotah became a forgotten backwater, a boom city that never was, a pointless outpost for a Georgia family come there by way of Texas.

Time and circumstance converged upon this part of the world to particular advantage during these early years. Although Checotah was bypassed by boom, the border region around it grew prosperous quickly and spread its bounty in unexpected ways. Being in the right place at the right time is an oilman's primary definition of luck, and Monty Mon-

crief would always attribute to divine grace his fortune in
having been born where and when he was.

Railroads were creating a new frontier in the early part of
the century as they crisscrossed the land. Their coming
meant the making or breaking of a frontier town, meant
boom or bust, and so homesteaders with a stake in the land
banded together to boost the virtues of their particular settlement in the hope of attracting railroad promoters. The
owners of what had recently been hog pastures and dirt veg-
etable patches could expect to find themselves big-league
landholders with city streets named after them if the railroad brushed by them right, so they used whatever means of
persuasion they could think of to make sure that it happened. The federal and state governments added to the fer-
ment; their policies encouraged westward expansion by
deeding huge unsettled tracts to promoters and dreamers
and schemers, who then sold them off to finance roadbed
construction. These men in the middle got rich in the process, but what is more important for this particular story,
they also gained control of access to the remote plains. And
so they made the transport of oil possible just when it was
first being discovered.

Railroads began to bring prosperity, and oil kept the land
rush going, opening up new settlements to the cycle of
boom and bust. The earliest American oil financiers were
often Easterners who controlled the railroad lines. The
Western boast *faster horses, older whiskey, younger women,
and more money* is variously attributed to railroad men who
came to Texas in search of oil and huge profits. It was not
unusual for railroad tycoons from the East to ride down to
Texas by private car and make deals on behalf of small companies that later grew to be majors.

Such men were essentially gamblers who staked their
money on real gamblers, lucky horse traders who won mineral leases in late-night poker games played by dust-bowl
farmers hungry for quick cash. With their pockets full of

leases, these back-country hustlers set themselves up as oil-men, acquiring the rights to adjacent plots and selling shares in whole blocks in order to finance their seat-of-the-pants drilling operations. Every aspect of these ventures was spec-ulative, for no scientific method of geologic testing had yet been devised, and such formations as twisted beneath the earth's surface lay entirely unmapped. Little besides in-tuition inspired these early transactions—intuition, and the optimist's faith in the future that has always prevailed upon the frontier. *No guts, no blue chips* has always been a wild-catter's expression of faith.

As it had encouraged the growth of the railroads, the fed-eral government encouraged the search for oil in order to promote Western settlement and so force the Indians into ever-further retreat. The policy of permitting landowners to retain or dispose of the underground wealth of their prop-erty was formulated deliberately to encourage expansion and development. Bureaucratic controls were reduced to a mere filing of papers, so that wildcatting might proceed unhindered.

And so it was the chance to make a private killing—in oil, in railroads—that drove men and women to settle the harsh expanses of the American West. The right to do whatever they pleased with their land thus became their first defini-tion of freedom, the basis from which all of their hard effort flowed. Of course this freedom existed by design of the government, which was deeding over land rights to suit its own purposes. But this irony went generally unacknowl-edged, and the paradox has continued to haunt the West since its first days of settlement.

"It all lay out there for the asking," said the pioneer, William Larimer, of the open frontier. He had founded a succession of towns across the West before making his final settlement at a crossroads of Colorado called Denver. And when Monty Moncrief came of age in Oklahoma, it all just lay out there for the asking too.

Sooners were arriving then from every state in the Union.
Stories of overnight success were being played out in bright
little jewel-like prairie towns like Ardmore, and in wide-
open lawless enclaves like Hell. A Western version of the
Horatio Alger myth carried the day, with all its attendant
optimism and innocence, and Monty Moncrief's own story
held true to its classic outlines.

He had the angelic stepmother that Texas legend seems to
demand; his first job was as a soda jerk. Like Lyndon
Johnson, he began life teaching debate in a shady little settlement after graduating from a teacher's college.
He went to France during the First World War, having
trained for the cavalry like a red-blooded Oklahoma boy,
but he found himself in the artillery division instead, there
being little call for roughriders to face down the tanks sent
forth by the arms of Krupp. And like so many young heroes
who left the artless towns of frontier America in those years
to make their first forays upon shores where the shadows of
men fell so darkly that it was thought only blood could wash
the land clean, the entanglements that enwrapped him there
did not dim the light of his native optimism. Perhaps among
those whose first twenty years had been passed in a land
large and open enough to free them from the rage of ri-
valrous conflict, innocence had taken too strong a root to be
destroyed by journeyings that might otherwise have sown
seeds of uncertainty.

In any case, Monty Moncrief remained untouched by the
ideas and doubts of a world he had fought for but would
never know, a world he would always call foreign. He retained his frontier high hopes through the years of battle
and waited for the day when he could go back home and
find a way to land himself in tall clover. On the bloody fields
of France, he befriended the son of an Oklahoma oil family,
and upon his return, he went to work for the young man's
uncle in Ponca City.

During the years between 1907 and 1928, Oklahoma was

the biggest oil producing state in America, and so in all the world. Oil lay shallow in this geologic province, known as the Mid-Continent, and the primitive oil-field technology of the time—low-rising wooden cable-tool rigs that punched holes a few thousand feet deep in the earth—was suited to its discovery. Wildcatters found a succession of "shoestring sands," long, narrow, intermittent deposits, across the length of prairies where the shoreline of an ancient sea lay buried. Layers and bars of sand had once been deposited amid the ooze of marine life here; as the ooze turned to limestone under the pressure of eons, the sands condensed into a coarser-grained sandstone, in the interstices of which particles of slow-moving oil lay trapped. The oil could not flow beyond the wall of denser lime, and so it accumulated in uneven scattered disks of sand, where nothing except intuition could suggest that a man should drill.

These Oklahoma shoestring sands proved rich. The Glenn Pool, the Cushing, the Healdtown strikes were successively the greatest of their day, but the suddenness of their discovery disturbed the normal rules of supply and demand in the marketplace. When the Cushing field came in, for example, the price of crude oil immediately fell to twenty-three cents a barrel. Gas stations began handing out free chickens in order to entice customers to buy it.

Twenty-three cents was hardly enough of a price to enable producers to make back their expenses. This fact encouraged them to pump their wells dry as quickly as possible in an effort to beat the falling price. As soon as the latest field was depleted, and the oil sold off, prices would leap upward again, until the next big discovery was made. The railroad men who controlled oil transport attempted to regulate the fluctuations by withholding supply, but competition made this impossible until John D. Rockefeller eliminated his rivals and seized control of oil deliveries across America.

Oilmen who were in it for the long run, who wanted to make one well pay for the next and that way keep drilling

for as long as they could, tried to band together in the early
Oklahoma days, to organize against the over-drilling of new
fields. But the business of wildcatting didn't take well to
such schemes. There was always some new horse trader
coming into the fields who wanted to sell as fast as possible
for whatever price could be had who undercut the competition. Exploration remained a laissez-faire activity, in which
anyone with the money or the trading sense to acquire a few
leases could join. Transport and refinery, however, were en-
deavors that lent themselves more naturally to monopoly,
and from such monopolies the major companies grew.

Of course the majors had not yet distinguished themselves
when Monty Moncrief entered the oil business after the
First World War. He began his career with one of countless
small companies, the Marland of Ponca City. He worked
first as a landman, as future independents often do. Landmen must acquire the mineral rights to property that their
companies want to lease from the farmers and ranchers and
timber merchants who own it, and so it is landmen who
develop those trading abilities that characterize successful
wildcatters as much as the indefinable instinct for sensing
where oil lies.

Landmen do not buy land. Rather, they lease the right to
produce minerals upon it from the land's owner, who takes a
share. A lease gives the operator—a company or an individual—access to a tract of land for five or ten years. If
oil is found before the lease expires, the operator may continue to produce it for as long as it lasts. If it is not, the mineral rights revert to the landholder, who may sell them to
the next bidder. The operator pays the landowner a yearly
rental fee on each acre for as long as no oil is found, but if
the land proves productive, he pays a royalty, a share of his
profits before cost. The share is usually one-eighth, and it is
called a royalty because it was once paid to the crown or the
state. It still is outside America.

The Marland was leasing land in the Texas-Oklahoma

borderlands during the years right after the First World War; that conflict had kept the demand for oil high throughout the years of boom and bust and so encouraged competitive exploration. Then the Marland had begun moving into East Texas, known to be a fertile zone ever since the great Spindletop well was drilled into a salt dome there in 1901. But the company had no particular interest in moving from the Oklahoma prairie until the early 1920s, when a North Texas booster named Amon Carter sponsored a gala for the American Association of Independent Petroleum Producers at his Shady Oaks Estate in Fort Worth as part of an effort to convince them that his city was the city of their future.

5

Where the West Begins

IT WAS "on account of the persuasiveness of Mr. Amon Carter," Monty Moncrief recalls, that his company moved to Fort Worth. It was on account of this same persuasiveness that many another independent came to that town during the 1920s, along with companies like Pure, Humble, Gulf, and Stanolind.

Amon Carter's efforts established Fort Worth as an oil town. No big strikes have ever been made nearby, and even shallow drilling did not commence in adjacent counties until after 1975, when high prices made it feasible. But Amon Carter, publisher of the Fort Worth *Star-Telegram*, once the daily newspaper for all of West Texas, was the very prototype of the Western booster, a man so determined to further his chosen town's fortunes that he shaped its growth to fit the outlines of his private vision. And Amon Carter's vision for Fort Worth happened to be oil.

They say Fort Worth is "where the West begins," and they say this not just because it sounds nice, but for a specific reason. Through Fort Worth passes the 97.20 west longitude, west of which less than twenty inches of rain fall each year. The unalterable fact of its aridity gives this land its harsh character, and it determined how it was settled. Those who ventured onto these plains needed far, far larger tracts of land than those who settled to the east: grasses were meager and it took many acres to support a herd of cattle. The size of the ranches brought forth great kingdoms, baronies ruled by masters of the plains. Of course these kingdoms extended under the ground as well as upon its surface, and for all that the sandy soil has proven barren, the many strata of sandstone and rich limy reef which underlie it are fertile, rich with deposits of oil. Cattle and oil then, products of this barrenness and this richness, are what define the economy and the way of life in the West, and because people who settled here have no choice but to live off these things, one may say with reason that Fort Worth is where the West begins.

Land boundaries, like the skies above, are neat and well-defined in West Texas, for they were established in an orderly manner at the time of settlement. The U.S. government gave land to individuals and to railroad companies, and the railroad companies divided their land and sold it off in neat packages. And so titles here are clear, unlike in places just to the east where conflicting periods of often-illegal settlement obscured a settler's right to his land and made dispute and consequent intrigue the rule. The people take their character from the land and from its way of being settled, and so while East Texans are often close-to-the-vest players, moved by the rhythms of backwoods intrigue, West Texans, much like the open skies and wide plains, exhibit a certain directness of manner. They are also tough, like the physical world they have mastered, and their dreams are large in proportion to their unlikeliness. Only true optimists and boosters could have settled this uncompromising and unpromising land; only optimists and boosters would have cared to.

Fort Worth was settled before the Civil War by north-
erners who hung signs on their doors like the one in Ohio
that read: "The country may be going to Hell, but I'm going
to Texas." The government was offering a bounty on buffalo
hides in order to deprive the Indians of their means of liveli-
hood; Fort Worth became a lively post for the bounty
hunters trade, and so the town flourished. But during the
war between the states, when the Union soldiers who had
manned the forts along the western frontier were called to
fight the secessionists, Indians—the Comanche, the Kiowa—
reclaimed the unguarded grasslands of North Texas, and the
settlements there were abandoned. After the war, however,
Fort Worth began to flourish and boom once again, this time
as a fording point and outfitting post for cattle drovers herd-
ing longhorns from South Texas north along the Chisholm
trail. Soon stockyard and slaughter pens and packing houses
were built, and Fort Worth became a prosperous trail's-end
stop. The railroads converged on the town—as many as six
different lines at once—in order to carry packaged meat to
the rest of the country. Maps drawn up by railroad companies and local promoters showed Fort Worth as the very
epicenter of American commerce, the focus of a spider's web
of transport lines.

Fort Worth prospered and grew. It became known for its
luxurious cattlemen's hotels, "palaces of the people," as
Daniel Boorstin has called them, erected before there were
even people to fill them, in the hope that they would bring
people to town; the speculators who built such hotels in the
early West were more interested in what they could make
happen than they were in fulfilling any need. Soon gaming
houses began to make downtown Fort Worth infamous as
"Hell's Half Acre," the hideout of famous cattle-rustling
gangs. Fantastic turreted mansions rose along the broad
new avenues, as cattlemen with half-million-acre spreads to
the north decided that a town house was necessary for civilized life. There are photographs that show the self-con-

sciously genteel social life that existed para~~d~~
Fort Worth's earliest and rowdiest days: yo~~u~~
dressed in white parade through the streets in flower-s~~tu~~
oxcarts, a crowd gathers at a "Japanese" party, to which
people wear elaborate robes and carry parasols. Young
wives, recently brought to town from the sod huts where
they'd started married life, sent to Paris for their dancing
dresses. Fort Worth, still raw with muddy streets and its fair
share of shoot-outs, was becoming a center of Western social
life.

But all these sudden flowerings of a frontier civilization,
set incongruously upon the bright windy bluff that crested
the Trinity River, began to crumble when the cattle business, following frontier tradition, moved on to greener pastures. With the advent of feedlot ranching, the cattle were
moved north to the vast flatness of panhandle Amarillo, to
graze and fatten for a year before slaughter. The packing
houses and then the railroads followed them there, and Fort
Worth suddenly lost its lively reason for being. The city had
been known as "Cowtown" throughout the early years of
this century, but by the 1920s, the epithet no longer applied.

For a while it looked as if Fort Worth might go the way
of other boomtowns that became a memory in the space of
ten or twenty years, and this might have happened had not
the exodus given an impetus to the rise of booster spirit, that
spirit which does not merely seize but also creates opportunity. It was this spirit that animated men like Amon Carter,
men who understood from the start that the success of their
frontier towns would determine their own chance for success in the world. In the half-settled West, there was no
reason for any one town to prevail over another, no inherent
suitability or innate "potential for growth" that made Fort
Worth or Dallas flourish while nearby hamlets like Birdville
or Lonesome Dove languished and died. Such things happened only because of the tougher efforts of single-minded
promoters who convinced railroad companies to lay tracks

through town, persuaded the government to dam rivers and create lakes where dry gulfs had been, conceived of grand hotels, created and named streets, invented whole new neighborhoods, and decided where highways should run. Such men and women gave shape to the land, and Amon Carter was one of them.

Amon Carter took it as his personal mission in life to bring the oil business—and later the aeronautics business—to Fort Worth to replace the cattle trading and meat packing business that had first made the city rich. He used the power of the newspaper he ran and his consequent influence over local businessmen and bankers to accomplish his determined ends. As a newspaper man, he stood in a good position for a booster, for local newspapers were among the most effective instruments of the boosterism in the early West. Indeed, many newspapers were begun in order to promote the growth of a town, while at the same time triumphantly declaring the town to be legitimate by virtue of its having its own press. Newspapers in frontier America began as advertising flyers rather than as ideological bulletins; news was secondary to their purpose, and because of their nonideological reason for being, their politics were nonexistent in the traditional sense. The only view their editors consistently espoused was the desirability of community growth. Newspapers made things happen on the frontier (as the great hotels did) simply by proclaiming a town's importance. As Daniel Boorstin has observed, the frontier press was truly pioneer, leading rather than following events, and representing things that "had not yet gone through the formality of taking place."

The Fort Worth *Star-Telegram* was such a newspaper. At one time, it serviced all of West Texas by means of the rural delivery system, and during those years the word "drought" was banned from the paper; West Texas, after all, was supposed to be a garden spot, and news of the infrequent rains that fell there might discourage development. Thus did the paper maintain a sort of fantasy vision of Western life, but that vision was no more fantastic than that of the man who ran it. Amon Carter styled himself as Mr. Fort Worth and affected the bizarre, flamboyant garb of some cattle baron that never was. He carried pearl-handled six-shooters, which he fired with wild ecstatic whoops into the streets of other cities during the travels he made to promote Fort Worth. He wore custom-made Western shirts, belt buckles fashioned from silver and gold, handwrought ostrich-skin boots, a beaver Stetson, vicuña coats. Everything was initialed, "personalized," then made in duplicate, in triplicate, a hundred times over and given as gifts to the victims of his relentless hospitality. Lyndon Johnson and other Texans in his mold would become famous for giving away tokens of themselves as memorabilia, as if they were tourist monuments themselves.

Through fat years and lean, Amon Carter ran his Shady Oaks Estate like a private chamber of commerce. There he courted the favor of those whose business he sought to bring to his hometown; there he sought to impress them with his private vision of life in the Wild, Wild West. Mules and longhorns grazed together on his private lawns, an incongruous echo of the peaceable kingdom. Near his house, he erected the cabin to which a party of local raiders once brought Cynthia Ann Parker to live as a respectable white woman. She had grown up among the Comanches and was the mother of the great Chief Quanah, and she fled from the cabin at the first opportunity. But although her story is one of spiritual victory for the Indians, it was presented on Amon Carter's lawn as simply one more heartwarming vignette in the story of the white man's struggle to subdue the plains, one more booster fable meant to give proof of Fort Worth's special destiny as a Western town. The settling of the West was of course justified by just such fantastic visions, and a faith in them testified to the strength of a settler's ambition. But with a man like Amon Carter, who so

thoroughly accepted the canon of booster mythology that he
self-consciously tried to incorporate its elements into his
own persona, it is hard to guess where the calculation of ambition left off, and the tyranny of obsession began.

Before prohibition, Amon Carter had bought up the entire
contents of the Casey-Swasey Wholesale Liquors warehouse
and built an underground bank vault with a burglar alarm
to hold the contents on the grounds of his fantasy estate.
And during prohibition, presumably by the grace of this
enormous supply, he began to practice hospitality as boosterism on a very large scale. In 1924, he invited the entire
membership of the American Association of Independent
Petroleum Producers to hold its annual meeting at his estate, just as he would later court the heads of companies
that manufactured airplanes and helicopters. From just such
booster efforts would Fort Worth's position as an oil and
later an air-flight center begin and grow.

And so it was on account of the persuasiveness of this
West Texas booster that Monty Moncrief, like many another
young oilman, left Oklahoma for the plains of North Texas
in 1924. Amon Carter, with the power of the press, could
make good on his promises to help oilmen out in times of
need. One of his advantages was that the old cattle estab-
lishment backed him in his efforts. Pappy Waggoner, for example, Texas's first billionaire, a rancher with interests
spread out across the north to the Panhandle, was always
willing to rescue an oilman down on his luck by using his
influence at the Fort Worth National Bank, the institution
that helped cattle barons in their early and needy days, and
would in turn help independent oilmen. During the Depression, for example, Pappy Waggoner was known to have written bank checks on his personal signature and given them as
unsecured loans to wildcatters who had had luck in the past.
And when a crowd of frightened depositors stood on the
steps of the Fort Worth National Bank in 1932 and demanded that they be permitted to withdraw their savings so

that they would not lose them if the bank closed, Pappy stood on the steps of the bank and asked the crowd to go home for the sake of Fort Worth: he promised he'd sell every cow and well he had if he had to, to cover their deposits. They went home. Supported by such determined and spirited early settlers, Amon Carter was able to shape Fort Worth into an oil town.

When Monty Moncrief came to Fort Worth, he brought his wife, an Arkansas girl named Mary Elizabeth Bright, whom he had met in Little Rock before going to war. Fort Worth was the kind of town to which a man brought his wife, and this distinguished it from the boomtowns and seedy frontier settlements to which few women came. Women performed a civilizing role upon the frontier to which many men had originally fled to escape the restrictions of civilization, a paradox that might help account for the ambiguity that characterizes the attitude shown toward them. For while their smallest efforts are accorded high praise—"I knew a man once during the boom who walked forty-six miles to visit a friend's home, just so he could see a home-like lady and the curtains she had made," an old oilman once recalled during a conversation—they really play no part in the world of men and commerce, with a very few exceptions. Their worth is judged by the dynasty they help to found and raise.

With his wife, then, Monty Moncrief came to where opportunity was open, to where it "all lay out there for the asking." He began leasing land for the Marland Oil Company all across the Southwest, working in partnership with a Dutch geologist. As a team they did very well, but they were working for a boss and so were never really satisfied. Monty Moncrief believed that he had a gift, a special talent for finding oil; he thought he might just have been born lucky. And so he itched for the day when opportunity would come his way and he could strike out on his own.

Then the stock market crashed. The Marland had spread

its holdings, speculating in stocks and bonds instead of
reinvesting its oil profits in oil leases, and so in 1929 the
company began to slide into an insolvency that undiversified
oil interests were able to avoid. Monty Moncrief decided to
bail himself out early, even though capital was hard to find.
He rented quarters in the old W. T. Waggoner Building, a
huge brick structure built by one of the great ranch over-
lords of North Texas, and set himself up as an independent
oilman. "I'd always had it in mind to better myself," he explains, and "to better himself" has ever been his quest. On
the frontier, self-improvement corresponds so unques-
tioningly to making more money that an equation between
the two is taken for granted.

When Monty Moncrief went into business for himself, the
Oklahoma oil fields were said to be dying, said to be all
pumped out. Such predictions have been made periodically
through the years, and continue to be made about one part
of the country or another, although new drilling techniques
—changes in "the state of the art"—continue to render the
forecasts premature each year. East Texas, however, was
heating up fast during the early postwar years. The great
fortunes of the first generation were being drilled out of
East Texas salt domes by men whose luck it had been to arrive there *sooner*. Their names and their discoveries would
give shape to all that followed. And so it was to East Texas
that Monty Moncrief decided to go, in search of a chance to
better himself.

6

The Daddy of Them All

EAST TEXAS, as Monty Moncrief would later declare, was "the daddy of them all." It was the old bull among geological provinces, where old bulls among men met their first big challenges.

There is nothing about East Texas that suggests wide-open spaces or a wide-open attitude; it is another world from the West. East Texas is a thick-grown piney-woods and post-oak country, shadowed with tall trees and blessed with rich black earth and wet weather. The land is inhabited by backwoods hog and cotton farmers and timbermen, and by drifters from the hills of Arkansas, a suspicious breed different from the cowboys and ranchers of the high plains. East Texas is also distinguished from the clear-horizoned West by its crazy-quilt pattern of land ownership, for it was not settled by an orderly advance of homesteaders preceded by cavalry. The province was a vital part of Old Mexico, which made no legal provision for colonization, and so it became a shadow district where land was often in dispute, a squatter's paradise. Its undefined duchies, often ruled by private vigilante power, lent their flavor of lawlessness and confusion to the oil business as it developed there.

East Texas is a wide-fanning arc of land that stretches between the Red and the Trinity Rivers and encompasses the rolling Sabine Valley; it is underlaid by salt domes and thick oil-rich sands that start and stop across its breadth. When oilmen speak of East Texas, however, they are referring not to the province as a whole, the humid third of the state that lies east of Fort Worth, but rather to the great East Texas field, a deep-buried thirty-mile sweep of sandbar that once supported 25,000 contiguous wells along its oil-rich horizon.

Just south of this fabulous formation, down along the Gulf Coast, the great Spindletop field was discovered at the turn of the century. It gave the province of East Texas, as distinguished from the East Texas field, its legendary name in the early oil business. Like most deposits of petroleum along the Gulf, the Spindletop lay along the crest of a salt dome. Salts had evaporated from the ancient seas that washed over the low-lying Gulf shores, and although sands and muds had washed over them, the salts sometimes grew hot from the pressures that disturb the earth and rammed their way upward in a molten state, like lava. When they solidified, these salts formed thick plugs that fractured the rock around them. Oil accumulated along the top and sides of these plugs, in the porous traps of fissured rock.

The presence of salt domes could be detected even when oil-field technology was in its most primitive state. Tasting the earth or the waters of nearby fresh-running streams will often indicate the presence of a salt dome. And because salt forms continuous structures beneath the earth's crust, domes can be charted by seismographic soundings. By the early 1920s, wildcatters had already learned how to shoot dynamite through solid rock and record the breaks that occur in the sound waves as they travel beneath the earth's surface. Such breaks indicate large discontinuities, where oil may lie entrapped. Thus it was that the earliest big discoveries were made near the Gulf Coast, where salt domes had formed.

The East Texas field, however, inland from the Spindletop and somewhat to the north, was altogether different. It was not the result of a structural anomaly within the earth that could be charted on a seismograph, but rather of random deposits left in the shadow of a retreating sea, compacted shoals of sand wedged tightly between ancient muds. There was no way of guessing its existence or gauging its extent except by drilling. The East Texas field qualified as a rank wildcat, and finding it during the deepest years of the Depression was a bit of pure luck that changed the fortunes of an entire state.

The oil-rich sandbars and lens-shaped traps of petroleum in East Texas lay in a 6,000-foot deep stratum known as the Woodbine horizon, which had proven productive to the north when the Oklahoma shoestrings were discovered. And so in 1919, a syndicate of Oklahoma oilmen decided to overlook the confusions presented by East Texas land ownership and speculate on cheap mineral leases there. As a rule, land with an unclear title is avoided by leasemen, who fear lawsuits from unexpected claimants upon royalty rights. But many of these particular backwoods properties were owned by Mexicans who had been granted land by the colonial administration in old San Antonio, or by Negroes who had sharecropped cotton upon it for the last hundred years, and it was generally assumed that these peoples' land titles could be manipulated easily enough by a group of Okie hustlers determined to open up the province.

Working alone among these men of the syndicate was an itinerant frontier scholar, a voluble yet reclusive quoter of passages from Shakespeare and the Old Testament named Dad Joiner, who had left his native Ardmore one day to pursue the dream that had long been his obsession—finding oil. Near the little town of Longview, Texas, Joiner managed to lease a few hundred acres, relying upon his own untutored

instinct that the land might prove productive, and upon advice of a sideshow artist-turned-geologist named Doc Single-
ton, whom nobody except Dad Joiner took seriously. Joiner
borrowed money from here and from there, and during the
early 1920s he went so far as to cut yellow-pine timber and
begin building himself a derrick. But he was soon forced to
abandon this enterprise for lack of money. He had no experience, only faith, and the syndicate backers from Oklahoma
did not consider him much of a risk, even in those feverish,
try-anything years. When at last he managed to sink a hole
in the ground in 1927, he drilled one dry well and then a
second.

But his third effort, a well he called the Daisy Bradford
Number Three in honor of the widow upon whose neglected
patch of scrubland it stood came in so rich that scouts sent
out to look at samples of the sand cored up from six thousand feet below believed that he had salted them with oil.
Dad Joiner's persistence vindicated his stubbornness, but his
poor head for business—and perhaps, in the end, his simple
bad luck—prevented his harvesting the fruits of his long labors.

Dad Joiner was so indebted to the banks and promoters
from whom he had raised his money that after he hit his bonanza, he had to sell off most of his leases in order to repay
his debts. He sold out to a much wilier trader, a man who
would make Joiner's rich acreage the keystone of his own famous fortune. The man was a gambler from El Dorado, Arkansas, and his name was H. L. Hunt.

"Everybody wanted to get a piece of Dad Joiner," Monty
Moncrief later recalled, "and everybody knew that he was
up for sale on account of his debts. But H.L. was as crafty
an old son of a bitch as ever was, and he sat on Joiner hard.
He had him locked up in the Baker Hotel down in Dallas,
and he worked on him day and night. None of us other boys
even got a chance."

While this was happening of course, drilling fever hit on

all sides of the Daisy Bradford. Wildcatters and companies big and small were leasing every acre they could get hold of at prices that rose with each passing hour. Every new well they drilled proved dry, however, and so it was very naturally feared that Joiner's field had been a fluke. There was no way of knowing then that the lens of sand in which it lay pinched out to the immediate east between layers of limestone ooze, but ran unimaginably rich and productive along a sharp slant to the northeast.

Monty Moncrief was still in Fort Worth during those first discovery days, stuck in the small time and wondering how he could bust out. East Texas leases were being traded in a fury at the old Westbrook Hotel just down the street from him, for the Westbrook was the customary haunt of every promoter who drifted through town. Monty Moncrief, however, disdained trading where those whom he didn't consider real oilmen could hustle their way in. He didn't see that he had much hope for getting in on East Texas until one day when a real-estate trader by the name of B. A. Skipper came around to the old Waggoner Building.

Fort Worth had acquired a reputation as an oil town by then, thanks to Amon Carter's skillful promotion. And so it seemed to B. A. Skipper as likely a place as any in which to try to unload the leases he held on four thousand acres near Longview, northeast of Joiner's well. No geological survey had been made of the land, but the acreage was cheap because Skipper hadn't paid off his leases. He'd taken them on open draft from the bank instead, hoping to get rid of them fast and turn a profit by doing so. Monty Moncrief thought it was possible that the Daisy Bradford might be sitting on top of a northeastward-running trend, and on impulse he bought the leases. To save himself money then, and to hedge his bet, he went partners with a man named J. T. Farrell, who worked down the hall from him. Then he journeyed out to East Texas, to add to his acreage and figure out where he wanted to drill.

Moncrief and Farrell didn't have enough money to permit them to expand their holdings and undertake the expense of drilling at the same time, so they did what independents have always done and sold off pieces of their enterprise. They gave up some of their interest to the Tidewater Oil Company, known afterward as Getty. Moncrief and Farrell held four thousand acres of East Texas land under lease, but Monty Moncrief had decided that he wanted to drill his first test well in a block of unleased acreage that sat in the very middle of his section.

Such open spaces are called "windows" among oilmen, and this particular window happened to lie in a forty-acre hog farm owned by a local doctor named Falvey, a stubborn character with a practice among black sharecroppers. Monty Moncrief employed his first days in Longview in pursuit of this man, sitting, as he recalls it, in "a room full of darkies," while Falvey took his own sweet time to think about his offer. At last the doctor informed his young visitor that he didn't want any oil wells messing up his hogs, and this put an end to the matter. Monty Moncrief went off discouraged, for from his first days with the Marland back in Ponca City, he had prided himself on his ability to make a deal.

He was taking his dinner that evening at the Gregg Hotel, a frontier structure erected hastily to accommodate the legions of leasehounds who had suddenly descended upon Longview. A man approached and introduced himself as Mr. F. K. Lathrop; initials rather than names were favored by many who made great fortunes in this part of the world. Lathrop was the owner of four hundred acres of scrubland the mineral rights to which Monty Moncrief had purchased from B. A. Skipper. Unlike the reluctant Doc Falvey, however, Lathrop was eager for his property to be drilled. He was so eager that he offered to split his landowner's one-eighth share of royalty rights with Moncrief and Farrell if they would agree to drill their first well on his acreage. Since there were no scientific means of knowing if one location might be more fertile than another, nothing except pure hunch and intuition to go on, Monty Moncrief accepted the deal and made plans to begin his explorations on Lathrop's spread of land.

The four hundred acres ran a few miles to the northeast of the famous Daisy Bradford, right along where Monty Moncrief had thought from the first that a sandbar might lie. His thought was nothing more than a guess, but his guess proved exactly right, and the first well he drilled gushed forth eighteen thousand barrels a day. Had he been able to lease Doc Falvey's land that first afternoon, his well would have come in dry, for the hog farm lay right where the sandstone pinched out into lime. This fortuitous twist further convinced Monty Moncrief that the good Lord must be looking out for him, that fate indeed had decreed it his lot to be an oilman.

Perhaps it is the conviction that one has been born under a lucky star that really leads to luck. In the oil business, where risks are high and only one well out of every ten produces, luck is the very essence of talent. It is thought of as a quality both natural and innate, something one is either born with or not, and a man will often stake another in his claim simply because he believes that that man is lucky. The extraordinary luck that has followed Monty Moncrief throughout his life first manifested itself in the East Texas field, and it adhered to him for the rest of his life, as if it were a tangible substance. Not long after the Lathrop discovery, he became known in Fort Worth, and indeed throughout Texas, as one of the greats.

Harry Sinclair himself, the legendary head of the Sinclair Oil Company and the big Eastern financial connection for the oil business in its early days, came down from New York to Troup, Texas, in his private railway car and courted Monty Moncrief and his partner Farrell. Sinclair knew that the pair would eventually have to sell out. No matter how many thousands of barrels their initial discovery well or those around it yielded, no matter how much money they made from them, two independents could simply never hope to develop the field that spanned their acreage by themselves. They could never command the resources to drill the hundreds of wells that must be drilled in order to exploit the structure of a major oil field.

This rule of the oil business was as true in the late 1970s as it had been in the old East Texas days. Even so wealthy an independent as Atlantic Richfield had to bring Exxon in to develop its discoveries in Alaska's Prudhoe Bay. A precise geometrical pattern of development and off-set wells must be laid out if an underground reservoir of petroleum is to be evenly drained, and these patterns can demand hundreds of millions of dollars. Such undertakings have proven beyond the scope of wildcatters from the beginning.

It is always a matter of time, then, before a wildcatter will sell off his successful discovery. But Harry Sinclair's time had not yet come when he arrived in Troup, Texas. His flamboyant efforts to woo Moncrief and Farrell went for naught. Monty Moncrief and his partner held onto their leases until the end of 1931, and they watched their worth increase many times. Finally, they sold out to the Yount-Lee Oil Company for two and a half million dollars. Yount-Lee used the property as the basis for a thirty-seven-million-dollar sale to Standard of Indiana several years later, a fact that would always rankle the wildcatters' hearts. But as Monty Moncrief always says, "in the oil business, there's no *what if*. There's only what happened."

In 1931, however, two and a half million dollars looked like pretty tall clover. And so Monty Moncrief returned to Fort Worth from the succession of boomtown East Texas hotels where he had lived while trading and drilling, and built the house across from the Rivercrest Country Club where he would live for the rest of his life. He could still hunt quail in the live-oak brush across the way in those days, for the house stood on the far undeveloped western edge of town, on the frontier. Frontiers of course do not last long in this part of the world, and already the woods were being cut down to clear the way for the homes of other men made rich by East Texas oil. The year 1931 might have been the deepest of the Depression, but millionaire's mansions were rising in profusion in Fort Worth, since East Texas and its environs had brought a sudden, great prosperity to the town.

The prosperity was based upon a tangible resource, and so it was not subject to the vagaries of rising and falling stocks. "Of course there were plenty of people who were living in shacks then, but oil has always made the big difference around here," explained a local man. He had married the heiress to a great contract drilling fortune, but he had once been a poor boy in town, and he can still recall the depth of wealth in those days. Once, he stood across the way and watched the ranch queen Anne Valiant Burnett Waggoner, drive her 1931 Duesenberg along the curving avenue that lead from her Norman-style chateau down to Crestline Drive. Unlike the oligarchs of New York and New England, rich Texans were not necessarily forced into diminished circumstances by the Depression, as the presence of Duesenbergs indicates. Texas fortunes had been built upon the bounty of the earth, and the memory of this advantage during a time of crisis has made many Texans mistrustful of paper fortunes ever since.

7

I'd Rather Be Lucky
Than Smart

EAST TEXAS brought a flood tide of oil wealth into Fort Worth, and into Dallas thirty miles to the east. Among those who came on the tide's crest were two horse traders from Athens, a pinewoods hick town some eighty miles from Dallas. Time and circumstance came together as luckily for this pair as they had for Monty Moncrief, and in time their long and separate shadows fell over the land as darkly as his.

Sid Richardson and Clint Murchison began life not as oil-men but as frontier hustlers. They were partners, and they traded cattle, horses, and whatever else came their way in domino parlors and hotel lobbies throughout the Texas-Oklahoma badlands. Perhaps it was inevitable that they should begin trading mineral leases, for both men were gamblers, and leases were a common medium of exchange among high rollers and low in those days. Many a poker player made desperate in the dead of a losing night staked the subsurface rights to the land from which he scratched a living in a game after all his money was gone. Like others of their generation, Sid Richardson and Clint Murchison won a place among the ranks of Texas's great oilmen because they knew how to play the odds and were very lucky. It was in gaming houses that old H. L. Hunt himself was said to have acquired the land upon which he made his first strike out of El Dorado, and many another frontier oilman found an El Dorado of his own because he drew ace high or held the wild card one lucky night.

When Sid Richardson and Clint Murchison began trading leases, they did so as promoters. They put together blocks of acreage and sold them off at a profit, retaining an interest in whatever wells might be drilled in the future. Like all promoters, they made money on the sale whether the wells came in or not. When they bought the rights to land on which the potential for oil was still untested, they were betting on their ability to find a buyer with greater faith in the land than the seller, counting on their talent to bluff. Sometimes they won and sometimes they lost, and the partners made and lost a few fortunes across the face of Texas before they went their separate ways.

Clint Murchison went to the woods of East Texas. Sid Richardson came to Fort Worth and settled. Whether he did so on account of the persuasiveness of Amon Carter or not is not known. His credo had always been that he'd "rather be lucky than smart, because a lot of smart guys go hungry." But for a long time, Sid Richardson was not lucky at all.

He did not, however, go hungry. For although he had been rich and gone broke a number of times during the great early days in Athens, he managed to maintain himself in high style even when his money was gone, and he continued also to drill dry hole after dry hole. He lived in bachelor splendor amid the heavy Edwardian comforts of the old Fort Worth Club downtown. He played high-stakes poker in the evenings there. Amon Carter, Mr. Fort Worth himself, the closest of his cronies, was generally regarded as the man who picked up Sid Richardson's tab whenever times were bad.

The two of them made a study in contrasts, for Amon Carter, always flamboyant, courted the limelight, dressing outrageously, firing guns into the night, posing for photographs and plastering his image all over the state. Sid Richardson—quite the opposite—stood in the shadows and covered his tracks; he was stout, dumpy, and determinedly plain. Amon Carter cultivated his own legend and sought to leave his tracings heavily upon the land, but in the end it was Sid Richardson who himself became the very image of the Texas-style wheeler-dealer, the billionaire behind the scenes who made things happen.

It was he, for instance, who flew to Paris to persuade General Eisenhower to run for President. It was he who spoke for the independents in Washington during the famous Tidelands debate, in which the federal government contested Texas's right to its offshore riches. And it was he who put the young John Connally to work as his lawyer in Fort Worth, using him as a liaison with Capitol Hill and with Houston. *Look* magazine featured him in 1954 as "America's Unknown Billionaire," and with the publication of that story, Sid Richardson became America's favorite insider's rich man, and Fort Worth the favorite insider's rich town.

Although it was not until his later years that Sid Richardson came into his enormous wealth, he always managed to put a deal together during the lean years. "He'd been lucky before," said a local promoter, when asked how a man could have managed to run a tab and find investors through a long bad spell. "Everyone just assumed he would be again, and they were waiting for his luck to turn." Monty Moncrief explained it in a similar vein. "Sid Richardson was an optimist," he said. "That gave people confidence." These explanations affirm the oilman's faith that luck—and the belief in luck—is a talent, a gift. If one has ever had it, it is assumed that one always will.

Manifesting a lucky air is of transcendent importance in this business of risk and hunch, and Sid Richardson's skill at doing so was masterful. It was an art he developed during long years spent perfecting a frontier gambler's best weapon, the bluff. Sid Richardson once told Clint Murchison that "I must be the richest one between us, because I owe more money than you do. They've got paper of mine floating all the way to London, England." And perhaps this attitude, as much as the presumption that his luck would eventually turn, was what enabled Sid Richardson to live high on the hog in Fort Worth while waiting for his luck to turn.

His was an attitude that found no innate shamefulness in going broke or in borrowing, so long as there was reason for it. And such an attitude is still necessary for an oilman, who after all must be reckless to some degree. "My daddy figured if he wasn't in debt, it must be because he wasn't aggressive enough," Larry Meeker, scion of a smaller Fort Worth oil family, once said. And the daughter of an oilman whose fortunes rose and fell throughout his life, a man who went broke several times but never thought of asking his wife to sell off her diamonds, explained it this way. "Here in Texas," she said, "everybody's part of some crowd. And if that crowd just happens to be the oil crowd, it's assumed that you're broke some years and flush others. You keep on living like you've always been living, and borrow when you must. There's nothing to be ashamed of in low times."

Such clubbiness, such transcendent concern for those who are part of the crowd, is characteristic in the oil business, which has always run on private arrangements and good-old-boyism. It is characteristic as well of the frontier, where fortunes are made overnight, and you don't cross the man who's driving the hog cart because he just might turn up owning half the county tomorrow.

But such clubbiness is perhaps more than anything else evidence of a stubborn sense of self-regard, the conviction of individual right and a lack of guilt over indebtedness. This absence of fear of disgrace is something that those who live punctiliously upon installment plans have had bred out of them. Timidity, of course, is something that those who take huge risks simply cannot afford, and it is perhaps the absence of any need to make apologies for the occasional big losses that sets independent oilmen apart, makes them seem like real men, successors to the range-riding heroes of Western history.

Their boldness exhibits itself with flair. The daughter of a Fort Worth oilman, for example, took pride in boasting of her father's habit of being in debt. "My daddy hated bankers," she recalled. "He said they never took risks, only bet on a sure thing. Once, he went over to Dallas to see a man at the Republic National Bank building about a loan, and while he was there he ran into another vice-president or something who'd lent him money before. The man said, 'I'm going to collar you before I let you out of here, Fred, and make you pay back what you owe us.' But my daddy just told him to go to hell—said he'd come there to borrow more, not to pay anyone back."

What this heiress's daddy knew how to do was call a bluff; bluffing is the optimist's secret weapon. Optimism is of course the personal quality that nurtures luck, and optimism was something that a man like Sid Richardson understood. Fort Worth's conception of him as an innately lucky man turned out to be exactly accurate, of course. He as much as anyone established the city's reputation as golden among wildcatter towns of the Southwest, confirming the vision of his old friend and crony Amon Carter.

It was the billion-dollar Keystone field that broke Sid Richardson's long run of bad luck and redeemed his faith in himself and the faith of his champions around town. The Keystone lies at the very corner of Texas, where New Mexico slices in to form the Trans-Pecos spur. The way it sits on the map just dares the adventurer to try his luck, and Sid Richardson was the man who called the land's bluff at last. He found some of America's richest reserves there in the late 1930s, buried eight-thousand-feet-deep in a lush layer of limestone compressed between undulating levels of shale. And it was by calculating the worth of these reserves that *Fortune* magazine accounted Sid Richardson the wealthiest man in America.

The Keystone was like an amulet, and ever afterward Sid Richardson would have the fingers of Midas. He went next into Central Louisiana and began the rush on that fertile part of the country; his golden touch led him straight to the great Iliona field there. It was in the Iliona that Perry Bass made his debut in the oil business. Perry Bass was the only son of Sid Richardson's only sister and the doctor whom she had married up in Wichita Falls, and he had been raised from birth to be his bachelor uncle's heir and successor. Sid Richardson had always called his nephew "son" and been a hero to him, but on the day that eighteen-year-old Perry Bass's real father died, all that changed. His uncle began to call him simply "Bass," and it was "Bass" from that day forth, bawled out in a tone that many recall as particularly humiliating. Sid Richardson could speak of his heir as "son" with all the tenderness of the kindly grandfather of Western legend when that heir was only a nephew. But as soon as the boy became like a son in fact, his uncle turned as tough as any old bull in this story, determined to give the young bull a hard time.

His first challenge to his nephew proved particularly wily and allusive. Perry Bass had gone to Eastern schools all his life, and to Yale after that. He had acquired a more refined accent and a certain gravity of demeanor that Texans schooled in the East often have. But when he finished, he came back home to Fort Worth, just as the son he would later raise to be his own heir would one day do. Upon Perry

Bass's return, his uncle demanded that he build for him a home on his own private island in the Gulf of Mexico, an island called St. Joseph's that lies off the spit of land between Port Aransas and the Cedar Bayou. The old man had lived in hotels and in the Fort Worth Club all his life, but now he wanted his dream house, and he proved exacting in what he required.

Perry Bass called the old man's bluff, and he saw the day come when Sid Richardson moved to his kingdom by the sea to breed Santa Gertrudis bulls, leaving his empire to the younger man. It was "by the grace of Uncle Sid never having married," Perry Bass was fond of saying, that he got into the oil business; his own interest was in the sea, in sailing and marine conservation. And it was by the same grace that the Bass family became one of Texas's famous, and the very name of Richardson seemed almost to vanish with their ascendance. For on the day that Sid Richardson died, Perry Bass turned the tables on the uncle who had suddenly begun to call him simply "Bass." He changed the name of his uncle's oil company to Bass Enterprises, and it has been Bass Enterprises from that day forth.

And so Sid Richardson's name is memorialized now only in philanthropic enterprise, through the Sid Richardson Foundation. His most visible traces may be discerned in the art museum that bears the name of his old cohort and inevitable rival, Amon Carter. The building, smooth squares of golden pumice shot through with the tracery of evaporated fossil life, stands in the rude Texas sunlight atop a gentle rise in west Fort Worth, seeming in its simplicity almost Greek. Inside the museum—silent, dust-free, cooled by air that smells like electric current—are ranged the paintings and the bronzes of Frederic Remington and Charles Russell that both Amon Carter and Sid Richardson collected all their lives, and which once hanged in their poker suites at the Fort Worth Club.

The spirit of their competition was marked by mutual secrecy and low-level intrigue. A dealer from Boston who sold to them both said that he had to swear to each man that the other had not seen whatever piece he was being shown, for each feared buying the other's rejects. Amon Carter perhaps had the better deal in the end, having secretly acquired the entire holdings of a Great Falls, Montana, bar called the Mint, where Charles Russell used to drink, much to the dismay of local citizens, who had hoped to keep the art in a museum of their own.

Among the hundreds of items thus acquired was "The Joy of Life," a peep show Russell had painted for the bar. Today, even this raunchy bit of frontier life lies entombed within the sober walls of the museum, pickling in the brine of air-cooled homage. The collected treasures of Amon Carter and Sid Richardson hang together now, giving the illusion of mutual concord and respectability. Like "The Joy of Life," the raw edge of frontier comradeship and rivalry that characterized their acquisitions has been blunted by the smooth respectability of a later, tamer era. The visible traces left by men such as these are more seemly than the lives they lived ever were.

In front of the museum, in west Fort Worth, a single mesquite has been planted. It looks feathery and full of grace, not at all like the tough stubborn pest it really is. And like the tree, the spirit of the old gamblers who won leases in poker games and domino parlors across the state still sends its sturdy, greedy roots deep into the ground in which it was planted. Down in the soil, in the underlying strata, there can still be discerned in Texas the sources from which the feathery refinements that manifest themselves today spring.

8

Getting While the Getting's Good

WHEN SID RICHARDSON went west and settled in Fort Worth, his old partner Clint Murchison went to the fields of East Texas.

The piney woods were booming in the late 1920s, after Dad Joiner and then Monty Moncrief delineated the East Texas field. The problems of glut and overproduction that had put early Oklahoma through a cycle of boom and bust were coming to some kind of resolution in East Texas. They had to, for the discoveries made there were so large that they threw the entire world's supply of petroleum out of balance. Controls upon the rate at which oil could be drilled were sought by some wildcatters, who wanted to stay in the business and see their sons follow them into it. These men saw no conflict between the frontier spirit and a little self-interested self-restraint.

Clint Murchison was not among their number. "Old Clint was one of the boys said to be running hot oil in East

Texas," Monty Moncrief later observed, referring to the practice of shipping illegal amounts of crude to covert refineries. But Monty Moncrief was only stating the obvious. Murchison had named his business the Liberty Oil Company to declare his open contempt for all efforts to regulate his business.

"Free ass, free grass, and to hell with the herd laws" had been the rallying cry of the cowboys who saw their nomadic way of life brought to a sudden end when the open plain was enfenced for ranching, and a variation on this rebel theme has sounded an echo through the annals of the oil business as well. The oilmen who first ventured north, south, east, and west across Texas in the succession of booms after Spindletop took their attitudes and traditions from the cattlemen who first claimed the land and fixed its character. And the cattlemen had defined liberty as an unrestrained grab for resources, let the future be damned.

Like the oilmen who would follow them, the cattlemen began as adventurers upon the frontier. They came west after the Civil War to round up the five million longhorns that roamed the brushy Rio Grande *brasada* and drive them northward along wide trails, where they could graze on virgin grasses six feet deep. Being adventurers, before whom all things appeared to lie open, untested, and free, these men did not consider too carefully what the consequences of their actions might be.

They did not care, for example, if their tough and rangy charges carried in their bellies the pods of mesquite, that stubborn pest which had infested Old Mexico and destroyed the grasslands there. The longhorns left these seeds behind in their droppings and so destroyed the pastures that they grazed upon. These pastures had made Texas a rich land of promise, but the men who drove the cattle northward were more concerned with their immediate push to market than with the wasting of the land. They knew that millions of fresh acres lay just ahead, waiting for them over the old worn-out hill.

Writing of *Texas Wild*, Richard Phelan noted how when a local botanist tried to instruct a group of early cattlemen about how to maintain and assure the continuing fruitfulness of the native grasses upon which their cows grazed, he was met by a declaration. "Resolved: none of us know, or care to know, anything about grasses, except we are after getting the most out of them while they last." The cattlemen's resolution might serve as an epitaph for the frontier attitude, which holds that there's always something better waiting up ahead. It was an attitude they bequeathed to the wildcatters who ventured onto the open plains in their wake.

Getting the most out of whatever it was for as long as it might last—that was most certainly the creed that prevailed in East Texas, where the mad rush to drill up every patch of leased land hurt the men who found oil there as surely as mesquite ultimately became the cattlemen's worst enemy. Consequences cannot be escaped when they have been built into the natural scheme of things. But in East Texas, consequences were not supposed to be taken into consideration. In East Texas, freedom—liberty—meant getting while the getting was good.

The big sandbar that described the East Texas field added greatly to America's oil supply at a time when there was already a glut because some Houston wildcatters had opened up the riches of Venezuela. The price of oil had always seesawed as new discoveries were made, but because East Texas produced in nine years more oil than all of Europe, Africa, and Japan ever had, it destroyed the market entirely. Discovery and production were competitive rather than cooperative undertakings, so although common sense indicated that slow development would benefit everyone, the frontier attitude worked against it. Those resolved to "get while the getting was good" continued to drill and sell as fast as they could, and every possible section of land was leased and occupied by a drilling rig. As oil gushed forth, sending up flares of rich gas to be burned off at the well-head, prices fell lower by the day. At last, they reached ten cents a barrel. Small wells were abandoned, others were capped, and all over the state wildcatters quit their search for oil.

Like the virgin grasses of Texas, the oil fields had only so long a life. Pumping them dry during a time of glut and low prices made little sense for anyone with an ongoing interest in the field. Yet those who had invested in East Texas leases had no choice but to drill, or to see the oil that underlay their land sucked up by faster, greedier drillers whose property adjoined theirs. The "rule of capture," which governs oil as it does game, designates oil as belonging to the land from which it is drilled rather than to that where it originates. And since oil lies in porous reservoirs of rock beneath the ground surface, and travels like any liquid toward wherever the pressure has been relieved, it takes the path of least resistance, and flows underground to the nearest opening. Drilling a deeper well next to a discovery will drain it dry, much as luring an animal will entice it from the land where it has kept its lair. The poaching of game by trespassers is illegal, of course, but no law prohibits the capture of an animal as it roams from one man's property to another's. Oil, like game, is migratory. Whoever can attract it by relieving the reservoir pressure may claim it.

The rule of capture forced even conservative leaseholders to drill like hell in order to prevent their oil from being poached. Undeveloped reserves stood in danger of losing pressure and fizzling in the earth if left there too long. Gas and oil are mixed in varying proportions in every pool of petroleum; gas provides the pressure that drives oil upward from its stratum of rock, into the pipe-threaded well-core, and out into the sky above. Gushers, those vaporous fiery geysers that shoot up uncontrollably from the ground, may look dramatic, but they are in fact disastrous, for they indicate that too high a proportion of gas is present in the oil. Not only must the gas be burned off and so lost forever when the well is brought under control, but whatever oil remains in the ground loses the expulsive force that gas gives it, and is quickly depressurized. Such wells are said to have been depleted. For although hundreds of thousands of barrels may yet lie in the rock below, the oil must be laboriously pumped and repressurized by chemicals at great cost if it is to be successfully produced.

In order to prevent overdevelopment and early depletion, the wells in a field must be evenly spaced, and each must be drilled at a slow and regular rate. In countries where mineral rights are held by the government or crown, and programs of planned production may be undertaken and enforced, this presents no problems beyond the inevitable ones of corruption. But in frontier America, even those controls that worked to the general good were considered contrary to the freedom, the liberty, that men had come west to find.

Settlers had acquired their acreage from government grants, of course, and railroads had been built with money raised by selling off public lands. Yet such contradictions were popularly ignored, for they went against the prevailing ideology. Unrestricted ownership of land and the unfettered right to dispose of its resources was the ideal that drove men and women to stake their claim upon the harsh wilderness. Any system of prohibition or threat of hindrance looked like a threat to the ideal, so even commonsensical restraints were feared.

Wildcatters—or some of them, like Clint Murchison—clung like the cowboys before them to the ideal of an absolutely open and uncontrolled frontier. They saw enforced regulation of the common good as the fatal beginning of state meddling in private matters, and they fought back hard with guns, defiance, and wiles. They built concrete bunkers around wellheads and hired armed guards to defend their turf from government inspectors. They smuggled oil across state borders in trucks purporting to hold something else. They operated unregistered refineries in backwoods bayous to process crude produced in excess of what each operator was allowed. Chaos and defiance ruled the day, and those who led the way made little secret of their refusal to be controlled.

And yet the ideal of complete freedom in East Texas was incompatible with reality. Unrestrained development worked against the common good. As a consequence, full and bloody battle broke out between gamblers and hustlers determined to get what they could from the land and move on, and the men who wanted to make the oil business continue into the century and be passed down to their sons. They understood that only some means of regulation could protect their future interests. The common good was a long-term form of self-interest.

The battle that raged between these opposing groups had its precursor in the fight between the cowboys and the ranchers who fenced in the open plains. At issue in that fight had also been the frontier definition of liberty. But unlike the earlier contest, the one that began in East Texas never reached a satisfactory conclusion. The lines of battle are drawn sharply even today between those who see limited regulation as essential and those who do not. And the old rebel yell of "free ass, free grass, and to hell with the herd laws" finds current expression in bumper stickers that read, "Drive ninety and freeze a Yankee."

Yankees generally appear in Texas legend in the guise of regulators, telling Texans what they can and cannot do. But of course it was not Yankees but the oilmen themselves—those in it for the long haul—who first brought regulations and controls into the oil business. The laws of supply and demand worked so badly during the East Texas glut that producers there first tried banding together to prevent overproduction.

They began by voluntarily limiting the number of wells that could be drilled, and they spaced the wells at regular intervals. Then they restricted the amount of free-flowing crude that could be taken from the earth. Those who supported these efforts considered themselves conservationists, and they were something new on the frontier. They refer to themselves as conservationists still, although the word has been usurped in recent years by many to whom the very existence of oilmen is an anathema, and who stand in opposition to them from across a gulf of misunderstanding and cross purpose.

But voluntary measures could easily be brought to naught by a single wildcatter who refused to comply with the rules, and such refusals were commonplace upon the frontier. With the East Texas field in chaos, the governor of the state gave the task of regulating the oil fields to the state Railroad Commission. It was then that the language of the bureaucrat was first heard in the land, the talk of each operator's allowable, of proration and rated potential, of off-set wells placed in symmetrical balance to allow for the even drainage of oil. It was a language that came in time to enrage oilmen and confuse everybody else, for it was an anomalous language in the dense piney borderlands, where even the simplest definitions of justice had been left hazy and undefined, and right had always belonged quite simply to the strongest. But it was a necessary kind of talk at the time, and to enforce its definitions, the Railroad Commission sent state militia and armed Rangers into the fields.

"Proration," the basis of all regulation, is a means of prohibiting each well in a field from producing at its full potential. The amount of oil pumped from each well is made equal; thus is pressure retained and the field's early and uneven depletion prevented. Oil and gas remain in the ground as reserves, instead of being drilled up all at once and stored in expensive tanks. Proration is a strategy for conservation, for giving long life to the fields.

Monty Moncrief was one of the conservationists who fought for voluntary controls in East Texas. He and Clint Murchison might both be seen as archetypes of the Texas oilman, but they are archetypes of very different sorts. Monty Moncrief appears in the guise of the grand conservative patriarch, driven by his fabulous luck to drill up the land and leave the tracings of his shadow across its horizon. His figure moves behind the scenes, magnetic and authoritative, but he is not given to making the aphorisms that render a character immediately colorful; he is content instead to let stories be told about him, about his toughness. Clint Murchison, quite conversely, epitomizes the brash, hard-living, big-spending wheeler-dealer. He was a public rather than a private figure, flamboyant and ostentatious, the man everybody knew. And he was never loath to toss off the outrageous lines that have made him memorable in the years that have passed since his death.

Both men made their first fortunes in East Texas, but both adhered to the different versions of frontier philosophy that prevailed there. Monty Moncrief's ideal was one of free enterprise in which cooperative measures are undertaken in a clubby spirit of good-old-boyism, and handshake agreements prevail. Murchison remained true to the basic creed of scrambling for all that could be got, and letting the chips fall where they would.

Their different philosophies sprang from their different loyalties. "We're strictly oil operators around here, one-hundred percent family-owned, unincorporated, and independent," has always been Monty Moncrief's boast. His family has always been in it for the long haul, so advocating a measure of conservation has been to their interest. Clint Murchison, however, urging liberty in its coarsest and most unfettered form, was always looking one step ahead. He made his great Texas fortune in oil, but his loyalty was not to oil but to whatever lay waiting on the open horizon. "Money is like manure," he liked to say. "*Spread it.*"

And "spread it" is just what the Murchisons have done.
Within the space of a single generation, they spread it all
over railroads and cattle ranching and real estate, and all
over the Dallas Cowboys, which the family owns. The Murchisons live in Dallas, and "spread it" has always been the
watchword of that town, which is why it is what it is today
—diverse, developed, Anywhere, U.S.A.

Fort Worth, thirty miles due west, is a different place entirely, for money there is not like manure but like oil. It does
not spread out but rather collects heavily in pools, coagu-
lating but not stagnating because of dynamic pressure
steadily applied. Money in Fort Worth deepens, thickens,
stays in the oil business and is plowed back into the earth,
which is why that town is in its turn what it is—distinct, lop-
sided, Texas without a doubt. The differences in their loyalties put Monty Moncrief and Clint Murchison on opposite
sides of the battle for control in East Texas, and the
difference has been reflected in their lives and in their two
hometowns.

The Murchisons' scheme of diversification—the Dallas approach—came to general attention when it was learned that
old Clint's sons, John and Clint Jr., had secretly acquired
control of the New York Central Railroad in 1964. To those
in the East long accustomed to assuming ownership of
fixtures of commerce like this one, the sudden discovery that
such a holding had fallen into such hands gave final proof
that a crass new class of wheeler-dealer had come to power,
proof that what was imagined to be a more gentlemanly
way of doing business in this country was about to meet an
ignominious end.

A second generation made invincibly rich by oil had come
to power, eager to spend and without scruples about doing
so. Years later, when Yemeni and Saudi investors began buying up banks in Houston and Atlanta, a similar note of alarm
was sounded, with Texans cast this time as the self-righteous
old guard, defenders of time-honored gentlemanly tradition.

But the Arabs, like Clint Murchison, simply knew how to spread it. They were taking the Dallas approach, and diversifying with riches claimed from the earth.

The Arabs knew how to spend it too, just as Clint Murchison had. In Dallas, people are more public about such things than they are in Fort Worth, and the Murchisons have come during the passing years to represent an extreme of the Dallas style. Stretched out past Highland Park, the leafy suburb of privilege that could be mistaken at the glance for rural Connecticut, lie the barren flats of North Dallas, a treeless and sun-baked expanse. Across North Dallas curl the tracings of several billionaires' rows, whose harshness mocks the more conventional beauties of the mere millionaires' neighborhoods to the south. For here, in plain proud view from the road, are ranged a variety of brick buildings— usually pinkish and low-roofed and enclosed behind camera-monitored gates—built extravagantly to look like motels, like office buildings, like ski resorts, like pavilions at Versailles.

Such homes, flung up like experiments on the edge of nowhere by those who, like desert sheiks, seem always to be preparing to move on, seem to play out some frontier ideal of freedom. From a cross-city expressway at the farthest edge of North Dallas, one sees the cold sweep of land that is "the Murchison spread" standing in magnificent isolation as if to fulfill every expectation of what a modern *Giant* should be. It has the look of a sumptuous frontier outpost, like the desert mansions outside Riyadh and Jidda, and like them it does not appear permanent, does not seem built to last.

The mansions of North Dallas are throwaways upon the scene, splendid but without even the trappings of substantiality, mirages, brief oases, stopping points on the way to somewhere undefined. As the city of Dallas continues to move northward, its millionaires' rows precede it, for millionaires place their bets on the edge of the frontier, and the city calls their bluff. The risk is always there, but as Clint

Murchison was fond of saying, "After the first hundred million, what the hell."

Of course diversification has taken hold in Fort Worth as well as in Dallas. The heirs of even so archetypal an oilman as Sid Richardson have learned to "spread it," to cut the odds. Bass Enterprises now owns hotel chains and real estate. And the suburbs that stretch west of town are changing, becoming more anonymous as money made from electronic gadgetry enriches recent arrivals. But the scent of oil still hangs in the air, and the families whose great wealth came from it still cluster in the arc of road that curves around the old Rivercrest Country Club.

Fort Worth is still a city of dynasties. And because the independents, like the cattle ranchers before them, were motivated to found dynasties to which their sons and their sons' sons could succeed, many of those who came to live in Fort Worth held with the more conservative definition of liberty, and refused to cry "to hell with the herd laws" when those laws worked to their eventual, long-term benefit. The new mood of defiance that has seized them lately, and which finds expression in the "freeze a Yankee" attitude, has gained impetus only as government regulations and laws have multiplied so thick and fast that they have begun to threaten the very dynasties they were established to create.

9

To Hell with the
Herd Laws

MOST of the great old Texas oil fortunes that were not first made in the piney woods of East Texas were made in West Texas, the vast expanse of mesquite-choked semiarid brush country that begins just west of Fort Worth.

The land there is sorry, as the people who live on it say. And it grows sorrier with every westward-moving league, although the clean blue overarching sky gives a dignity to the empty wastes, and the passing of clouds across it creates a day-long drama. But the land is rich below its barren surface, underlaid by double and triple layers of oil-saturated sands. These were formed first by coral reefs deposited on the floors of ancient seas, and then by the buckling of a vanished mountain chain, the Marathon. Marine life, under pressure of metamorphic change, dissolved into petroleum, which now spreads out under a full four-fifths of West Texas.

During its days of early settlement, West Texas was

deeded out in large, evenly defined spreads. Enormous tracts were necessary to support cattle and sheep ranches here where the grasses grew sparsely. The neat boundaries, wide spaces, and clear land titles made this an easier terrain to exploit for oil than the jumble of East Texas had been. And the succession of depths at which oil lay, moreover, assured its continued development. Monty Moncrief, for example, although he was too young to catch the first boom, got in on the second, which followed it by some thirty years. His discoveries added immeasurably to his first great East Texas fortune.

Just as the piney woods gambling dens of borderland East Texas gave a certain rich flavoring to the oil business as it developed there, so did West Texas define its character further. West Texas, more than anywhere else in America, was settled by optimism, pure booster spirit, by the willingness to go on faith and instinct, to believe that hard work and the taking of high risks must inevitably bring reward. Perhaps only something as stubborn and unreasoning as faith could have inspired men and women to settle and remain upon this harsh unyielding land. Whatever the reason, the optimist's equation of faith with eventual success left a mark on the oil business from the earliest West Texas days.

The first West Texas wildcatters were optimists without equal. They had to be. In the years before the First World War, the U.S. Bureau of Mines had begun issuing a series of pessimistic surveys, estimating that 40 percent of America's petroleum reserves had already been exhausted, and concluding that the domestic oil business was not far from dead.

West Texas oilmen refused to take these reports at their word even though no oil had ever been found in their part of the country. Finally, the Catholic wives of one group of promoters appealed to Saint Rita, patroness of impossible causes. They strewed rose petals upon the saint's statue

early one morning at church before their husbands ventured
forth upon a bleak hog ranch where instinct had told them
oil might lie. The men drilled their first successful well then,
and they named it the Santa Rita Number One.

A mining engineer for the Texas and Pacific Railroad, a
man so tough and laconic in true high-plainsman style that
even his family referred to him simply as "Mr. Gordon,"
held a similarly stubborn faith. He had been sent by his
company to oversee operations at a little crossroads known
as Ranger, formerly a command station for Texas Rangers
defending the land from fighting Comanches. Soon after arriving in this barren land, Mr. Gordon convinced the railroad to send a geologist down to look for oil on some property it held.

The geologist studied the land and concluded that drilling
in West Texas would be a useless waste of company resources. But in 1917, in the middle of a severe drought that
heralded the dust-bowl era and forced farmers to abandon
their land and head north, Mr. Gordon took the opportunity
to lease up 300,000 acres of sorry ranchland himself for almost nothing. He hauled in a big rotary drill, and almost
overnight the dirt farmer who owned the land was making
$200,000 a month in royalty payments.

The town of Ranger became the site of the greatest frontier "gold rush" of all time. It was ten times the size of the
strike that brought the forty-niners through icy mountain
passes to Northern California, and five times the size of the
Klondike. The gold this time was liquid of course, and lay
trapped within Permian shales, but it lay just shallow
enough, just close enough to the surface, to bring to Ranger
the frontier gamblers and vagabonds and unaffiliated
traders who followed the booms and who made them. From
across America came men who could hustle up a few dollars
and drill oil that didn't lie too deep.

In their wake came the professional boosters and optimists who spoke of growth as an inevitability, something

divinely ordained. Some who came were second-generation frontiersmen who'd begun their lives in hovels and had nowhere to go but up. Others had abandoned the comforts of Eastern cities in hopes of making quick fortunes in this far, ugly corner of the world. All were possessed of a frontier faith that the sacrifice of immediate pleasures would bring inevitable rewards. And all sought to wed their fortunes to that faith by encouraging growth.

Growth meant railroads. Ranger was the first West Texas boomtown not only because oil lay beneath it, but also because the railroad ran through town. Other rich West Texas fields had to be shut down after they were discovered because there was no means for hauling derrick parts in or shipping barrels of crude out to refineries. But after the first discovery, the rush to lay tracks began. The get-rich-quick heyday of West Texas became a bonanza for railroad schemers as much as for wildcatters.

Until the Ranger boom, the vast sweep of land from San Angelo—the central sheepherding capital of Texas—to the tumbleweed gravel pits of New Mexico had been almost uninhabited. But no sooner had oil been discovered than three different private railroads were racing to lay the first tracks from Fort Worth to the little villages of West Texas. Each promoter competed fiercely to convince gamblers that *his* railroad and the towns springing up along it were indeed the wave of the future, the true cutting edge of the frontier.

Boosters of those towns sent brochures out across America, proclaiming the mesquite-choked sands where rattlesnakes, tarantulas, scorpions, and coyotes preyed to be a prudent field of investment for the "sapient seeker of opportunity," a "Mecca for practical pilgrims" who traversed the desert in search of the great West Texas Allah, oil. Money poured into towns before a single stone had been laid. Hopes and expectations were for all or nothing.

But despite rich promise, the scene that met the dreamers and schemers who came to West Texas was a harsh one.

Men slept in tents pitched upon the freezing desert floor, or crowded into blanket rolls in shacks instantly turned into hotels. Brutal theft rings were organized by men who had been rustling cattle only a year before. Mass ptomaine poisoning from rotten food broke out. Wild bucking burros loaded with equipment bogged down in mud when sudden rains turned desert dust to a swelling torrent. All the discomforts peculiar to cities born overnight on ungoverned backlands were here made worse by a climate predictable only in its violence.

Such harshness put to the test the willingness of people to put aside all thoughts of present comfort and pleasure and live exclusively upon hopes for the future. This ability to delay gratification is perhaps more than anything the definition of Puritanism, the spirit that animated Western settlers as much as it did any group in history. The Puritans who settled New England's rocky coast had had this same stern ability to ignore their present circumstances and live upon their hopes, but they had been sustained through hardship by their passion for free worship. Frontier settlers had instead of the hope of heaven only the hope of a pot of gold as the reward for hardships endured.

And so their defense of the right to earn money took on the character of a religious faith, and as the harsh land brought them suffering, so did they imagine themselves entitled to its fruits by a kind of divine election. Anthony Trollope, traveling through the central states in the late Victorian era, remarked in missives sent home to the London newspapers upon the madness of civilized men and women who chose to live in caves. But the madness he wrote of was as old as America. It was a madness that found full expression in the Western boom.

Many of the families that helped establish Fort Worth as an oil town made their first fortunes in Ranger, and so they brought with them the harsh character of West Texas and its wild optimistic faith. Typical among them were the

Meekers. Larry Meeker—the man who recalled the toughness of the father who made him leave law school and come to work for him, but who cried unashamedly when speaking of his grandfather-hero—is the oldest son of the present generation. A younger brother named Bill, from whom great things had been expected, had by his late thirties already made a huge fortune and become the protégé of several older oilmen, the husband of several fabulous West Texas oil heiresses, and the sweetheart of a few others, but he was killed in a plane crash while still in his prime.

Bill Meeker died during the same year that two other successful young third-generation wildcatters also died in freak accidents, one from a broken neck, another who burned to death when his backyard barbecue pit ignited: sudden violent deaths of favored sons are oddly common in Texas towns like Fort Worth. The youngest Meeker son, Jim, had taken to living mostly near Santa Fe, where he studied the Bible, practiced philanthropy, and talked of drilling in the burning red Sangre de Cristo mountain range if he ever got it all together. And so it had been left to Larry Meeker to carry on family tradition as best he could.

"My granddaddy was born in a hole in the ground," Larry Meeker was fond of saying, "and you can't start life much lower than that." His grandfather had been a carpenter who brought his bride to a sod cave in the Texas Panhandle. He worked odd jobs and followed prosperity all over North Texas, and when the Ranger boom began in 1917, he and the sons who were old enough journeyed there in search of their fortunes.

He went to Ranger with the idea of building shanties for the fortune-seekers who had begun arriving there from every part of the globe. But he and his sons soon learned how to barter their skills in an eager and open market, and after a few months in West Texas, they returned to the Panhandle with twenty thousand dollars in cash and some solid interest in mineral leases as well. "We ain't carpenters now, boys," Larry Meeker's grandfather said, "we're oil-men!" And upon returning, he immediately moved his family to Fort Worth, the big city for those who had made their money in West Texas oil strikes and were unwilling to delay the gratifications of civilization any longer.

The carpenter and his sons were able to parlay their small percentages into larger shares, and soon they controlled a substantial interest in some of the great West Texas and New Mexican fields. They lived close to the bone, however, following the frontier oilman's practice of sinking profits from the last well into the next one and taking pride in debts, which gave proof of venturesomeness. Some years they were flush, and other years they smoked turkeys and made "Meeker's Mustard" on their Fort Worth farm and sold these products for cash. But like Sid Richardson and other optimists' sons who had their ups and downs, the Meekers remained inside the charmed circle of Fort Worth's oil world, and were protected through good years and bad.

And indeed, the cohesiveness of that world is demonstrated by nothing so much as the Meekers' present position within it. For a run of bad luck in New Mexico and the Panhandle coincided with depressed gas prices and the flood of foreign oil into America in the 1950s and the 1960s, and although the carpenter's descendants never abandoned the family business—never joined the three-quarters of all independent oilmen who went out of business during those years—they found their properties considerably diminished. By the time Larry Meeker took over the business which his father had warned would be his only through death, the company was participating in just a handful of wells each year. What was once a West Texas dynasty had been reduced to the single suburban office of Meeker and Company. Larry Meeker was running it alone.

A sign hangs on the door of Meeker and Company that reads, "If You Like the U.S. Postal Service, You'll Love Nationalized Oil," and this sign pretty much defines Larry

Meeker's attitude toward life. Bureaucracy, government interference, the creepy-crawly octopus arms of Washington,
D.C.—Larry Meeker blames these things for having destroyed his family's business and the frontier way of life. He
spends much of his energy decrying the insidiousness of a
system that he believes has destroyed incentive in America—
the kind of incentive that allowed his grandfather to tolerate
life in a cave in hopes of building toward something better.

He devotes hours to staging his own complex protests
against that system. During the spring when his neighbor
Dick Moncrief was drilling like hell in the Gulf of Suez, for
example, Larry Meeker occupied himself with an elaborate
plot of revenge against the Internal Revenue Service, which
he claimed was auditing him because he had produced from
one well more than its quota of gas during November; it had
rained all during October, he explained—what did they expect him to do? He kept his juices flowing by planning to
disguise his profits from a Mississippi well by trading the oil
for Mississippi plywood, the plywood for Florida orange
juice, the orange juice for shoes manufactured in Ohio, the
shoes—the scheme turned circular, its logic vanished, a fury
had seized Larry Meeker. "*Damn* trying to convince the
poor foolish people of this country that there's some kind of
oil shortage and then suing oilmen for producing instead of
shutting in their wells," he shouted. Tears began to fall from
his strange, hurt blue eyes, eyes set prominently in a handsome but tired-looking face. "I love this business, I love it, *I
love it*," he said, "but the bureaucrats want to see it destroyed. They can't stand the way my daddy did business."

Larry Meeker had previously described his daddy as a
tough old bull, out to give the younger man a hard time and
make him suffer. But when he recalled the way the old man
did business, he felt compelled to enshroud his virtues in a
mist of sentiment, deeply felt but with an air of myth about
them. For the frontier of Larry Meeker's imaginations has in

fact not vanished from Texas at all, although the Meeker family may find itself in lessened circumstances just now.

Yet nostalgia and the sentimentalizing of the past is not uncommon in the world of Texas oil, where people feel the tenor and the sympathies of the larger world running in a current against frontier idealism and the all-powerful will to conquer. And Larry Meeker's spirit of resistance, his ceaseless garnering of examples of government interference and official pessimism, his categorical equation of unrestricted enterprise with freedom and liberty and everything good in America, put him in a direct line of descent from Clint Murchison and all those who have ever cried *to hell with the herd laws.*

10

A West Texas Superlative

BILL MEEKER, Larry Meeker's dashing younger brother, had confounded pessimism and conquered nostalgia for what his grandfather had done by going directly to the frontier and making a great fortune of his own. He had disdained his old bull of a father's insistent command that he join up with him, and had gone to Midland instead. In his defiance, of course, he had shown something of his grandfather's true spirit. For like the old carpenter who went to Ranger, and like so many other of the third generation who have occupied themselves more with cultivating their own brand of optimism than with remembering the deeds of those who have gone before them, Bill Meeker found that he was simply *not content*.

Ambitious third-generation oilmen often go to Midland to make a name for themselves. Perhaps they go in order to show that they can endure the modern equivalent of Texas frontier life, and thus prove themselves worthy to carry on family tradition. Or perhaps they go because Midland is where the men who once rushed off to Ranger would go today to get in on the boom. In Midland, possibility still seems to exist without limits. It's a West Texas optimists' town.

Midland rises up suddenly in the midst of a monotonous, almost lunar expanse of gray clay flats, strewn with tumbleweed and the rubble of erosion. Its incongruous towers, modern minarets, appear almost to float in the shimmering heat, enchanted and unreal, like a mirage. There is nothing likely about Midland's existence, no reason for it to have become a trading center or even to be where it is.

And indeed, Midland would still be just one more mesquite thicket had not a frontier optimist named Ben Hogan built a twelve-story office tower in the midst of the desert back in 1929 and named it the Midland Petroleum Building. No deposits of petroleum were known to lie nearby, so there was no conceivable need for an office tower, but Ben Hogan believed in the future of Midland, and he figured belief could see his vision through. He managed to persuade nearby settlers to underwrite the cost of his dream tower, convincing them to believe in the future too. It was not until oil was discovered in Midland County during the prosperous years that followed World War II that Ben Hogan's faith would find final vindication, and scores of new towers would rise up from the vastness.

Midland, born only because of a dream, is the most West Texas of cities, and the most Middle Eastern as well, for it is a walled and towered and a richly planted city. West Texas wind storms blow sand into ears, nose, eyes, and hair, and doors must be sealed against it, and each plot of land fortified by barriers. Within the city's walls, terraced lawns and tropical plants are tended with obsessive care, as if the determination to make exotic species of vegetation take root and flourish were spurred by the very difficulty of making them do so.

In Midland, one hears as much about a family's hothouses as one hears about its millions, those millions being almost taken for granted and sometimes as easy to come by as perfect, heavy blooms. And in Midland, one sees more clearly than anywhere how women still play out their roles as bearers of civilization upon the frontier. Cultivation is always the first act of the civilizer, and in the desert, civilization means orchids and roses, means trees that give shade and fruit. Sequestered inside Midland's walls, women make the desert bloom, while men stand watch in the towers.

The harshness that necessitates walls and makes of gardening a fierce competitive enterprise is transformed into an "ideal climate" in the booster literature that relentlessly promotes Midland, and this too makes it the most West Texas of towns, the apotheosis of the booster village. In Midland, the optimistic rhetoric of advertisement takes over, and the depiction of the dream erases reality.

Just so was reality contradicted in the scores of "bird's-eye view" lithographs which in the nineteenth century depicted settlements that were really no more than dirt crossroads as grand flourishing frontier villages. But then Midland is a dream city, an oasis, like Mecca. And like Mecca, it is the final stop along the caravan trail, although the caravan that passes through is comprised not of camels but of cream-colored Eldorados and Sevilles, twin-engine Cessnas, and Silverados with four-wheel drive. Midland, like all of West Texas, is a place of promise for nomads who, like the Arabs before them, have traveled across the desert sustained by their faith. That their faith has as its object the hope of striking it rich does not diminish its power to inspire.

Midland's golden age, which made a whole new generation of Texans rich all over again, began after World War II, when the Humble Oil Company struck oil in the rich Pennsylvanian reef. Its rich deposits of marine life had been laid down a full fifty thousand years before the Permian red-bed shales in which the first West Texas discoveries were made. The Permian fields, which had brought men to Ranger and inspired the furious building of railbeds in the wilderness, had lain shallow, close to the gravel-scarred surface of the West Texas earth. Drilling them had presented few problems, once the right sands were found and the equipment hauled in. West Texas wildcatters simply drilled until the gas lost its pressure, and then they moved on.

The Humble discoveries, however, opened a new technological frontier. For the Pennsylvania fields were drilled right under the old depleted formations by rigs that spun with a smooth rotary motion. The rigs employed the new Hughes tool bit, that rock-solid triple-toothed cone which replaced the delicate fish-tailed steel bit and ground the earth's rock to powder instead of hammering it down. Upon this single piece of metal, a vast paper empire was soon to be built.

The new oil lay deep, but there was money and incentive enough to take advantage of the new technology in the prosperous, unregulated years directly after the war. The Humble fields opened West Texas up again, despite official proclamations of pessimism. The optimists came back into the fields once more.

Monty Moncrief had been operating since the days of East Texas along the Gulf Coast, in Arkansas, and across Central Texas. And although he continued to be successful, he could not be said to have lengthened the shadow he'd cast in his glory days. The new West Texas boom was going by without him, just as the East Texas boom had once looked like it would. But then, as had happened before, that "little element of luck or the good Lord looking out" to which he has always attributed his success came looking for him. This time, it came to the Santa Anita racetrack.

He had gone to the track with his wife, who had acquired a taste for the horses and was a regular there during the couple's visits to Palm Springs; Monty Moncrief did too much gambling in the oil business to be diverted much by the races. He was approached at the gate by a geologist from Dallas named Paul Teas, who asked if he had been fol-

lowing the fabulous Scurry field play then being made in
Snyder County, West Texas. Teas had some leases there that
he wanted to sell for $60,000. Monty Moncrief had heard
about the Scurry, just as he had known about Dad Joiner's
play in East Texas before his big chance came to get in on
it. And as in East Texas, Monty Moncrief acted quickly
when opportunity presented itself to him. The day after
Teas cornered him at the racetrack, he agreed to buy the
West Texas leases, and offered another $100,000 to enlarge
the acreage. Teas would be given one-eighth interest for
having brought him the deal, and he could buy an addi-
tional one-eighth from Monty Moncrief if he chose.

After making the deal, Monty Moncrief broke his long-
standing prohibition against bringing outsiders into the oil
business and hedged his bet by offering equal quarters to his
Palm Springs golfing partners, Bob Hope and Bing Crosby.
They were always wanting to get in on an oil deal, he later
explained, and since this one had come his way so easily, he
decided to share it. They agreed to the price and went partners with him and Paul Teas—each man paid $40,000 for a
share in the leases, and Monty Moncrief added $80,000 to
drill the well.

"It came in dry," he recalled, "and I'd say those Hollywood friendships came in dry too." For although Monty
Moncrief drilled twenty-eight straight producers on the
Scurry field holding after that and returned $5,000,000 to his
partners on their $40,000 investment, he claims that his part-
ners wanted nothing to do with him after that first loss. He
attributes this to their inability to understand luck, which
amounts to a simple impatience and lack of faith. "Here in
Texas," he explains, "we know luck is something you wait
for. You stick by somebody until he gets lucky here. Maybe
that's the kind of thing Hollywood teaches a man to forget."

The Scurry field deal added luster to Monty Moncrief's
legend. Because of the partners he brought in with him, rumors spread that it was he who had brought the big film

stars into the oil business. He was even said to have been
the man who persuaded Jimmy Stewart to use the profits
from his most successful film to back the Shenandoah Oil
Company of Fort Worth. Of course Monty Moncrief had
nothing at all to do with the founding of that famous little
independent, which in time became the principal developer
of petroleum in Guatemala; Monty Moncrief's attentions
were engaged by Moncrief Oil exclusively. And his West
Texas experience soured him forever on taking into business
with him friends that moved in circles outside Texas oil,
men accustomed to dealing by contract rather than staking
their word as their bond.

Whatever his partnership problems, it was the fight he
waged to get the very best from his West Texas fields that
finally distinguished Monty Moncrief's strike there, and inspired him to boast about it in terms that his grandson
would one day understand as a challenge: "We made the
greatest deal that could be made in the world at the time,"
he said.

The Humble Oil Company, formerly the little "fly-by-
night Burkburnett outfit" so like a thousand others in West
Texas, was by 1948 well on its way to becoming the giant,
many-tentacled Exxon. The company was expanding, and
after the discoveries it made in the Pennsylvanian reef, its
officers sought to unitize the field, to produce every inch of
acreage themselves and then pay the leaseholders who already held title to a proportion of the profits. Unitizing was
a cooperative measure first undertaken in the East Texas
days. By permitting a single operator to distribute wells
evenly across an entire field, this practice eliminated wasteful drilling and prevented the early loss of gas pressure that
had plagued the fields.

The largest leaseholder usually operates a unitized field;
in the case of Scurry, this was the Humble. But Monty
Moncrief was not satisfied with what the Humble had to
offer him there. The twenty-eight wells he had drilled lay at

the periphery of the field, so when the oil was flooded out of
the formation through the central crest, their value was
diminished by the drainage. Independents are rarely willing
to jeopardize their relations with major companies by taking
them before regulatory boards, but Monty Moncrief
brought Humble to the Railroad Commission and began to
make things difficult for the company.

He was trying to save his deal, of course, to get a fair settlement for wells being dealt short because of their position.
But he was also trying to vindicate his earlier efforts at pro-
moting conservation in East Texas. He had, after all, disdained those oilmen in East Texas who'd cried "to hell with
the herd laws," and he had labored to control acquisition by
private means instead. The wisdom of his earlier position
came back to work for him in West Texas, for the Railroad
Commission ordered the Humble to compensate him for his
fields, and the contract they agreed upon was something he
could boast of as being the greatest in the world at the time.
If the price of oil had remained the same, it would have
taken the company thirty years to recover the hundred million dollars along with percentages and residuals on those
percentages that it agreed to pay Monty Moncrief.

"We aced the Humble in Scurry," Monty Moncrief said,
counting the strike as a victory for his dynasty and a means
to its perpetuation. After all, the regulations he had fought
to have instituted were written with the idea of perpetu-
ating private dynasties, were they not? The day would
come, it was true, when Monty Moncrief would have to
admit that the Humble aced him, caused him to lose hundreds of millions through a few days' delay. But that day lay
in the future at the time the West Texas deal was made, and
it could throw no shadow across the optimism of a West
Texas superlative.

11

The Deal That
Got Away

"MAKE NO MISTAKE ABOUT IT," Dick Moncrief said
years later. "You look all your life for a Jay. It takes you
through a lot of bad winters. The trouble is, of course, most
people never find one."

Monty Moncrief, after forty years of almost continual
good fortune, had the luck to find a Jay.

By late in 1969, the price of oil had risen to three dollars a
barrel. The increase had come slowly, almost penny by
penny, over the course of the last decade. It had kept pace
with the gradually ascending price of Middle Eastern oil,
which three years in the future would begin tripling and
quadrupling as the Arabs took control of their own resources. The oil boom would really start then. But by 1969,
the business was already beginning to show fresh signs of
life. The new price on oil was inspiring even oilmen who
had long since left the business to go and hunt for their bonanza, their Jay.

Such hunts, as so often has happened, were undertaken in the face of official pessimism and gloom. As in the early days before the big West Texas strikes, the government geologists occupied the years preceding the new boom by broadcasting cheerless reports that domestic oil and gas reserves were almost entirely depleted. But such forecasts were rendered ridiculous in a very short time, just as they had been in West Texas. The Jay field, struck deep in the piney backwoods of the Florida Panhandle, proved the second richest vein of petroleum on the North American continent in recent years, after Prudhoe Bay in Alaska.

The Jay was Dick Moncrief's first big venture into the domestic oil business with his family, an auspiciously timed beginning that would prove typical of his luck. He had already made up his mind to challenge family tradition by taking his business abroad one day, but at that time, in his middle twenties, he had neither expertise nor experience to put in the service of his ambitions.

But the Jay provided temporary scope for even his large ambitions. And it remains something of a classic in the annals of oil, a story which, like the Israeli Deal, might be said to have all the elements: sharp trades and intrigue in isolated swamps, close deals made by closer friends, billions lost by last minute delays, the evening up of an old score between an independent and a major, and a vast payoff vindicating stubborn faith. No initiation could have been more perfect for a young bull on his way to becoming a legend, although Monty Moncrief, the old bull who made the play, always accounted it a partial failure, a deal that got away.

The Jay field lies in the timberlands of the western Florida Panhandle, just short of where the Escambia River cuts across the Alabama border. The sandstones are known as Tuscaloosa here, and they run all through this part of the world, for they were formed by deep-buried sandbars wavewashed against now vanished shores which arc through the Gulf of Mexico. Men had drilled the Tuscaloosa sands in

Florida for years, but had always found that this far east it ran dry, too compact to allow oil to form.

One man who had chased the fertile lengths of the Tuscaloosa was Marshall G. Young, the old wildcatter who had bought out the fabulous West Texas Rosier-Pendleton Oil Company and made it the basis for his great fortune. Marshall G. Young lived just down the road from Monty Moncrief, and like so many other independents in Fort Worth, he had a string of sons who followed him into the business, sons who were Dick Moncrief's friends and contemporaries. The Youngs had looked for Tuscaloosa sands in Florida all through the 1960s, and they'd bought mineral leases from pinewoods natives eager for a little cash. But their drilling ventures had met with failure, for the Tuscaloosa here was not about to yield any oil.

It was in the late '6os then, during a game of golf, as he now recalls it, that Monty Moncrief offered to undertake two-thirds of the Young family's costs in Florida in return for a two-thirds interest on their leases. He was the man, after all, who had mapped out the limits of the great East Texas field, and he knew something about the Tuscaloosa, which was called the Woodbine in Texas. The Youngs, grown weary of their chase, which had run its course through inauspicious and unprofitable years, agreed to his offer, and the Moncriefs took over the business of drilling. They began then to throw their own money down one dry hole after another, and soon they too grew convinced that the very sands, which had proven so rich to the west, were dead and dry beneath the Florida soil.

Nothing except drilling could confirm this suspicion. Deposits of oil are most often found in pools that lie atop or alongside deep-buried anticlines, those huge upfolds of rock shaped by the forces that rumble the earth, for oil is light and travels steadily along an upward grade. Geologists study seismographic pictures of these underground formations; the pictures do not show oil traps, but they can never-

theless be used to draw structural contour maps of how sub-
terranean rocks are layered and bent, and thus indicate
where pools of oil might lie. But such pictures aid only in
discovering oil as it lies along the slope-sided anticlines that
undulate grandly through the earth's core. Seismographs do
not reveal the small and sharply faulted formations cut by
ancient shorelines and buried reef bands such as underlie
the Gulf Coast. These can be located only by trial and error
drilling. New wells in such fragmented sands are always
rank wildcats.

The oil that finally gushed forth so richly in the Jay field
was discovered exactly where the Tuscaloosa had been
drilled by the Youngs and the Moncriefs and countless wildcatters before them. But the well was struck much deeper,
in the Smackover, a stratum of ancient marine sediment in
which evaporated fish fossils had been compacted into limestone porous with gassy debris.

The Smackover was a perfect bedrock source, rich with
decayed matter, but the particular formation that proved so
rich in the Jay lay along the downward slope of an anticline,
where oil, as a rule, never lies. A sandbar had intruded
across the top of the slope, so that no seismograph could
have recorded its presence. Monty Moncrief, however, had
noticed a knoll, a slight ridge in a tiny corner of his Florida
leaseholdings along the Escambia River, and the knoll
suggested to him that faulting or upheaval might have taken
place. Guessing that an oil field might lie below the dry
Tuscaloosa, he set about acquiring all the mineral rights he
could get his hands on. He spent a million dollars doing so,
and set off a fierce competitive buying boom in a part of the
country that had just begun to get hot.

Duane McDaniel, the Moncrief's landman, was sent
ahead as a scout, and to do the initial lease buying. He
rented a motel room in Brewton, Alabama, for two years in
order to accomplish his task, and he lived there alone.

The scent of intrigue hung heavy in the thick pine forest

air during those years, and as Duane McDaniel ventured
forth each day to dicker with dirt farmers over the price of
their acreage, he felt the eyes of his competitors trained
upon him. Information about who was buying what from
whom sold for a premium, and a man could hardly walk into
a country store and ask for a cup of coffee without his movements being watched and reported upon. Duane McDaniel
kept his own eyes open, using a backroad bait shop as a listening post from which to keep current of local gossip, but
in even this remote purlieu he knew that he was being spied
upon, and he discerned movement even among the loaves of
packaged bread. Being, like many landmen, a garrulous type
who delights in any circumstance that will provide him with
a store of anecdotes for the future, Duane McDaniel took
joy in his clandestine mission to Florida. He leased up land
everywhere he could.

As wildcatters and speculators got the idea that the Florida Panhandle was about to happen, the whole place started
to sizzle. Royalty rights went from sixty to six hundred dollars an acre, in a matter of months, and after the first discovery well was drilled into the Smackover, the price went into
the thousands. The Moncriefs managed to spend their million early in the game, however, and they were in on the
bottom floor. After most of the leasework had been completed, Monty Moncrief himself came to town.

He came in order to calm everybody down, according to
his grandson Charlie. Charlie is Dick Moncrief's younger
half-brother; he had just graduated from college when the
Florida leasing was at its hottest, and his grandfather prevailed upon him to be his chauffeur in Florida. Charlie recalls how his grandfather would hit the floor when another
car passed his Cadillac on a remote backcountry road; he
feared that if word of his presence got around, prices would
go as high as the sky.

One morning, the two men went to an old tin-hut café
near Brewton to have breakfast, and Monty Moncrief told

his grandson to get himself a newspaper. The young man replied that he did not feel like reading, but his grandfather told him again, "*get yourself a paper*," and so he did. He remembered the time when the older man declared himself capable of whomping the head of a rebellious child on the cement without compunction. The two of them then sat down to their ham and eggs, barricaded from recognition by the papers they held up in front of their faces, and they were watched by a dozen pairs of eyes that peeked over papers likewise upheld. The story of such intrigue, spread by an enthusiastic Charlie, became in time part of Monty Moncrief's legend in Fort Worth, repeated over and over like the B.L.N.T. narrative. For it was a story in which the patriarch was portrayed as acute, astute, and canny, the typical hero of Western myth.

"Granddad just came in and took over," Charlie Moncrief recalled. "He makes all the big deals, just goes in and tells them it's W. A. Moncrief. So even if it's a major company, what can they say? They have to hop to."

But Monty Moncrief was not in Florida just to make them hop to, to arrange the details of the deal and decide where the first well sunk into the Smackover should lie. For this particular venture marked the start of a new era in his family business, an era in which two of his grandsons would participate. Monty Moncrief's own son Tex, a man as private and self-contained as his father is genial and self-assured, had been with him from the time he came of age and had followed the older man's path without dramatically extending or challenging anything he had done. Tex Moncrief had come into his maturity during the bad years in the oil business, of course, and the men of his generation rarely had any choice but to be overshadowed by those who had gone before them. But times were beginning to change just as the Florida play was getting underway. And the two sons of Tex's who, as Monty Moncrief said, "got wet behind the ears" in that state, shared some of their patriarch's openness. One of them shared his fire.

"Dickie thinks of himself as the big deal man, like Granddad," Charlie Moncrief explains. "I'm more like my dad. I just want to do what's got to be done, and not always feel like I have to make a big hit with everybody. Dickie followed Granddad right from the start—he's real careful about that."

Charlie Moncrief is the oldest son of Tex Moncrief's second family. Even in his appearance, he differs from his older half-brother in much the same way that Tex differs from his father, for Charlie has inherited Tex's hunched stature, while Dick Moncrief shares his grandfather's regal sportsman's bearing. Charlie wears boots and jeans, but Dick Moncrief has adopted the sharp and careful tailoring that is his grandfather's trademark. Charlie likes being country, and Dick Moncrief's studied perfection provides him with some occasion for good-humored mockery.

But then it was never Charlie's ambition to be like Dick Moncrief. Herbie, who was older than Dick Moncrief, had been Charlie's idol; Herbie, said Charlie, was wild. But Herbie, the second oldest of Tex Moncrief's children, was one of those Fort Worth favorite sons of particular promise and great general popularity who met a shocking and violent early death. On his first night back home from Marine boot camp, Herbie was killed on his motorcycle on a long winding country road outside Fort Worth.

After Herbie died, Charlie decided to quit college and join the Marines himself. He had been spending time down at school in Austin, enjoying himself and drinking a lot of beer, but his brother's death signaled that the time had come for a change. The Marine Corps gave him the best time of his life, for he managed to become a squad leader without anybody being able to attribute it to his being a Moncrief. That was nice, because Charlie Moncrief was seeking a kind of anonymity he'd never known in Texas, and never would know if he went into the oil business, which he had every expectation of doing.

Charlie wanted to go into the Marines like Herbie, but his eyesight was bad. When the Marine Corps refused to send him overseas, he left and returned to school, studying more seriously than he had before, and he became a geologist. After he graduated, he joined his family as a matter of course. He did odd jobs in Florida first, and then oversaw drilling operations up in Wyoming and around the Utah salt flats. It was wild, rough, pioneering country, and Charlie Moncrief loved it. His dad, he said, had always favored the land up there too. And like his father, Charlie Moncrief was content to join his family and accept his lot, content to follow without challenging the way that had been paved for him by family tradition.

After Monty Moncrief came to the Florida Panhandle, spending a quick million to acquire mineral leases and royalty rights there, he began to make plans for drilling a wildcat deep into the Smackover. The first well site would be drilled into a small plain that was formed upon the floor of an ancient lagoon. At this particular point in the woods, several ridges fanned out, suggesting to Monty Moncrief a downward twist in the earth's subsurface.

The land on which this particular conformation lay belonged to the St. Regis Paper Company, which used its pine forests for timber, but had leased the mineral rights to Humble Oil, then in the process of becoming Exxon. Humble agreed to farm its acreage out to the Moncriefs and their partners, the Youngs. A farmout is an arrangement in which one company agrees to explore for oil on another's acreage, and pays the original leaseholder a percentage of the profits. Such deals are common between major oil companies and independents, because the majors lease up millions of acres just to keep as reserves, while the independents own less acreage but drill more wells. The incentive for the majors is that they usually must pay yearly rental fees on any land that is leased but not drilled, but can transfer their costs when they sublet the land. The St. Regis acreage had lain neglected for a long time when the Moncriefs came along and picked it up.

There happened to be a shortage of rigs at the time, because business was just starting to flourish again after twenty quiet years, and therein lay the rub. The Moncriefs were forced to delay their drilling plans for several months, and wait for a rig to be shipped in from Louisiana; the Smackover lay deep, and an especially big rotary was needed. The delay made everybody nervous. Having spent a million dollars on mineral rights already, Monty Moncrief was eager to test his new theory about the Smackover depth. He would not, however, sign his contract until he could guarantee a drilling date, even though not signing gave the company an opportunity to change its mind. Independents, dealing among themselves by means of handshake agreements, are often spared such worries, but major companies deal by contract, and anything can happen.

In the case of the Jay, it did. A few days before the rig from Louisiana was scheduled to arrive, a clerk in Humble's Florida office discovered that the company was committed to pay rental fees upon the land whether they drilled it or not. Farming it out in order to avoid payment therefore made no sense, and so Humble cancelled the deal before the contracts were signed. The company kept possession of the prime acres that the Moncriefs wanted to lease.

Humble went ahead and sunk the wildcat well. It was named the St. Regis Number One and drilled deep into the Smackover limestone on the site that Monty Moncrief had scouted, right where the earth's ridges fanned upward. The discovery opened up the Jay field clear across the length of the knoll. Because of their early lease buying, because of Duane McDaniel's country store intrigues and two years spent alone in Brewton, the Moncriefs held plenty of rich adjoining acreage. And when Humble unitized the field, di-

viding the profits among the leaseholders and producing the
entire field themselves, the Moncriefs took 4 percent of the
whole as their share. Had they not lost their original deal,
they would have had nearly 60 percent of this, the greatest
strike in decades. Perhaps billions of dollars had been lost
by the delay, but of course many millions were made.

The field's scope ran beyond anyone's expectations: three
hundred million barrels of oil were produced. The Smackover also yielded three hundred billion cubic feet of gas,
which came unexpectedly, as a bonus. Nobody was actively
searching for gas in those days; the interstate regulated price
of seventeen cents a cubic foot made it unprofitable to produce. "We were only looking for oil," Dick Moncrief explained. "It was up to three dollars a barrel at the time, so
you could think about making some money, whereas gas
meant nothing. With oil, we kept talking about what if the
price ever went to five dollars, but we never even saw five
dollars. It went right on past that, and took off straight up
from there."

The Jay's richness became the stuff of legend in Fort
Worth, especially since Kelly Young, one member of the
family that had brought the Moncriefs in on the deal and
had taken just a small percentage, was just then undertaking
to build his pink Roman-style villa on the far west side of
town. It became "the house that Jay built" in local legend, a
reminder of past glory that seemed also to presage the coming boom.

The Jay proved to be Monty Moncrief's greatest strike,
but he has never accounted it as his greatest deal. It was, on
the contrary, a loss by his standards, since so much of it had
slipped from his fingers through last-minute circumstance. It
wasn't losing the money that really mattered, since after a
certain point such things become academic: as Clint Murchison had said, "after the first hundred million, what the
hell." What bothered Monty Moncrief was being so close to
so great a deal, and seeing it get away.

"The Humble aced us in the Jay," he said, just as he'd said that he'd aced the Humble in West Texas. "We got out with a share, but if we hadn't lost our deal, *it would have been the world.*"

Monty Moncrief, when he speaks of his business, speaks in terms of "we." He says he doesn't "tolerate any of that *I* stuff around here." But when he speaks of the Jay, where his grandsons joined him for the first time, he is likely to break his own rule. "Did they tell you I was the man who started it all?" he asked a visitor who had mentioned the Florida field. He removed a heavy chunk of shiny black-green dolomite from a drawer in his office desk, and handed it across the room. "I was there the day the Humble spudded in, and when I saw that juice . . ." Monty Moncrief closed his eyes, and considered his loss. "If I'd made it through on that one," he said, "I could have put on my derby hat and walked downtown." When he opened his eyes again, they shone dark and clear for all his many years. "But in this business, there's no *what if*. There's only what happened." He concluded, "Just an unlucky roll of the dice, I guess."

12
The Last Elephant Shoot

MONTY MONCRIEF spoke of *the world*, and how he had lost it in the Jay. Dick Moncrief would stand alongside a cattle guard on his family's ranch property one hot spring afternoon and speak of *the world*, and how his family thought they had taken it in Central Louisiana. "It was like six blind men looking for an elephant," he said, alluding to the peculiar conformation of Tuscaloosa sandbars that spattered through the region. "We just opened fire and sprayed our shot. We were lucky we hit anything."

Central Louisiana—a swampland bayou region long considered unproductive even though it lay wedged between the old reliable Shreveport fields to the north and the fabulous offshore sands to the south—was brought in by Monty Moncrief as he was entering his eighties. Despite his seeming imperviousness to the passing years, he knew it might possibly be his last really big play. And because he was not the sort of man to go out with a whimper, he knew this deal would have to be something special, something with class. It at least had to match what he had done in West Texas. And it had to cast a little shade upon the Israeli Deal as well, for his grandson had already begun to bring that monster in.

Central Louisiana had been the brainchild, the obsession, of a Houston geologist named George Bouline. Bouline had gotten the idea in the early 1970s that a series of sand pods must have been built up along the leeward side of the coral reef that arched through this part of the world when it still lay underwater. The arch was a northern continuation of the fabulous Golden Circle reef, which proved so rich off the Mexican Gulf Coast. A Greek wildcatter named George Mitchell had discovered a number of these pods scattered throughout East Texas, and had struck deep pools of oil drilling into them. His strike was famous as the Seven Oaks play, and George Bouline had gotten it into his head that the Seven Oaks might serve as a blueprint for a whole string of sands along the reef. He wanted to test his theory in Louisiana.

The time was not yet ripe to do so, however. George Bouline had passed the 1960s and the early 1970s in the employ of major oil companies, among whom intuition and hunch are held in low regard. Like most Texas oil geologists, he had been unable to find work with an independent during the years when the domestic business fared so poorly. And so he had taken a job with a big company, which provided him with security and a big salary, but did not give him the freedom to use his imagination and test out new ideas. And so when the oil boom came along, he, like many of the best geologists, seized upon it as an opportunity to quit his job, and go to work for an independent.

The desire to work for an independent is partly a matter of incentive. A big company won't pay a good geologist four times what all their other geologists are making just because he discovers a two-billion-dollar field. But an independent will cut him in for a share of the profits. "The big companies have personnel departments which hire Ph.D.s just out of geology school. They pay them low salaries, and then count that as a savings," says George Bouline. "They think every quarterback is just a quarterback. They don't know you have to hire guys who are *lucky*."

The desire to work for an independent is also, of course, a matter of being independent. A big company will rarely trust a geologist's instincts if they don't fit in with some long-range plan of their own. Shareholders demand an accounting, and wayward hunches don't look good on the books. Bureaucracies place small premium upon uninhibited imagination. "Anybody who's got an idea of his own has to be a little bit crazy," says George Bouline. He's a straitlaced, decidedly unflamboyant scientist, who seems as far from crazy as any human being could be, but he's talking about a quirky mind given to flash insights about the nature of porous limestone. "Being crazy is something the majors just don't understand."

Major companies have all the technical advantages. They have budgets that permit them to speculate on leases and buy land in the hope that lightning will strike, company-owned rigs that prevent costly equipment delays, and private crews of geophysicists to do seismic work and map out likely strata underground. But imagination is what independents have always had, along with the freedom to risk everything. That's why they find 80 percent of the oil and gas in America, despite the fact that most of the mineral leases they acquire have been rejected by the big companies. "When you look at a major's stuff," explains George Bouline, "you know it's all cull. You're looking for diamonds in the junk heap, so you've got to be smarter than anybody else."

As always in the oil business, it all comes down to a question of luck, and Monty Moncrief's deal in Louisiana was lucky if nothing else. George Bouline had been unable to interest any big company in pursuing his sand pod theory, for although the majors had long been engaged in leasing Central Louisiana mineral rights as a speculative venture, exploring the unproven sands was of little interest to them as long as there was so much money to be made abroad. Traditional wisdom had always deemed that this part of the world was dead, and repeated drillings had confirmed it.

But when the oil business started heating up again, George Bouline went to work for the Moncriefs, and they gave him all the freedom he wanted to chase sand pods. His chance coincided nicely with the new economic situation, for until 1973, chasing the Seven Oaks would have made no practical sense, even to someone convinced of its imaginative plausibility. The reason was simple. The Tuscaloosa stratum in which the sandbars lay was rich with gas, not oil. And gas just wasn't worth producing during the years when its asking price was set by the government at seventeen cents per cubic foot.

The Tuscaloosa lay deep, at 18,000 feet. The first well Monty Moncrief drilled in Central Louisiana cost $4,000,000, and took a year and a half to complete. It yielded 7,500,000 cubic feet of gas a day, but that gas could be sold for only $.17 a foot. At that rate, Monty Moncrief figured that the well would be almost dry before he began to realize a profit. "We couldn't even think of drilling until gas hit two dollars," said Dick Moncrief afterward. "It hadn't actually gone to that when we set pipe, but we bet on the come." At $2 per thousand cubic feet, the well yielded $15,000 a day, enough to pay back drilling expenses within six or eight months. "That'll give us eight or nine years worth of profit," said Dick Moncrief, "which at fifteen thousand dollars a day is plenty. But you have to remember that the odds on hitting this wildcat were about fifty to one in the first place."

George Bouline's association with the Moncriefs coincided not only with a change in the economic climate, but with the family's sudden, lucky acquisition of 80,000 acres of rich Central Louisiana bayou lands as well. Gulf Oil had just finished drilling nineteen dry holes in a row in the area, and decided to abandon all further attempts. Phillips Petroleum, which held acreage adjoining Gulf's, was beginning work in the North Sea and had lost interest in the volatile Tuscaloosa. So Monty Moncrief began farming acreage out from these two companies, assuming all exploration and operating expenses in return for two-thirds of whatever profits he might make from the land.

Duane McDaniel, the landman who had spent two years of his life in a Brewton, Alabama, motel room, buying up acreage in the Jay field, worked on assembling the patchwork of leases that the Moncriefs acquired in Louisiana. Duane McDaniel, who spends his time trading anecdotes with farmers and landholders all over America, talking always in order to win their trust and with it the rights to their land, is a gregarious and a sentimental man. He cherishes the dramatic moments in life, and says he sees a poetic rightness in Monty Moncrief's late-life Louisiana elephant hunt, because the Tuscaloosa sands into which he was drilling lie in the exact same horizon as those in which the old man made his first great strike, the East Texas Woodbine sands. The full circle has come round in the course of a three-generation career, and Duane McDaniel can talk with poetic vehemence about such ironies.

He can also talk with poetic vehemence about lease-trading practices in Louisiana, which are as mixed up and unpredictable as a local gumbo with secret seasonings. Louisiana has retained to this day the peculiarities of the old French Napoleonic Code, a legal system based not upon the successive court decisions of English Common Law, but rather upon a series of statutes laid down, originally by the monarchy. Under this system, land titles present a variety of confusions, not least among them the "law of prescription," which returns mineral rights to the land after ten unproductive years. Such complications add to the landman's task, requiring that mineral claims be traced back just as land rights must be. Such complications also offend the sensibilities and natural prejudices of those who have taken as their motto the claim that "Land Is the Basis of All Wealth."

Private, unobstructed right of land ownership is as much an article of faith to the frontier entrepreneur as the freedom to make action; indeed, it is the prerequisite of all that follows. "Private ownership means incentive," says Duane McDaniel. "Take away that right and you take away all incentive, you destroy everything around you." As is his habit, he elaborates within a religious framework. "Developing the land is a matter of proper use of God's resources, his blessedness," he says. "Private landholds are man's covenant with God."

Incentive, in this scheme of things, comes near to being a holy thing; those who would hamper it are devils. But although Duane McDaniel has come to regard the search for oil as an almost religious quest, it was not piety that first drove him to become a landman. "I guess I liked the 'follow me' aspect of land work," he confessed once during lunch at the old Fort Worth Club downtown. "What I wanted was to own land and cattle, to be a big West Texas rancher. But it didn't take me long to see that my daddy hadn't set things up like that."

Duane McDaniel's daddy, a navy doctor from the outlaw side of Arkansas, had settled in Fort Worth and become friendly with the Moncriefs there. He sent his son to work on their Colorado ranch in the summers, and the boy decided then that he loved the life of a cattleman. But the ranching frontier had long since closed: raising cattle had become a vocation for ranch-family heirs and a rich man's hobby, particularly in dry West Texas, where many thousands of acres were needed to maintain grazing lands for a substantial herd. Duane McDaniel needed to make a living, and so he decided to become a geologist.

He graduated from college in the late '50s, just as experienced geologists had begun losing their jobs because so many independents were going out of business. So Duane

McDaniel took to the road and became a landman, hiring himself out to scout mineral leases all over the Southwest. While he was doing some roadwork between Kansas and Oklahoma, living in motels or sleeping in his car, he received a call from Monty Moncrief, asking him to go to work for the family. Since Monty Moncrief had "raised him up from being a pup," as Duane McDaniel says, he abandoned his independent ways. And after enough time in the Moncrief's employ, Duane McDaniel was able to realize the dream that began when he was working for them as a boy, and purchase a spread of Parker County ranchland and start raising Herefords of his own.

Perhaps it is on the strength of this realized ambition, and because he has been able to wed his fortune to his faith so well in the late boom years in Texas, that Duane McDaniel's faith in the American creed of optimism has developed such a strong evangelical strain. For he sincerely appears to believe that the forces which have been putting a greater degree of control over land into the hands of the state, fettering it with restrictions—environmental, archeological, zoning—are the very forces of darkness, whose design it is to smash man's covenant with God. His private version of the Apocalypse is born of his pride in having seen his optimist's faith fulfilled, and it is his conviction that those who would work against such pride are courting disaster.

Like Max Banks, Duane McDaniel does not look at undeveloped land as unspoiled wilderness, evidence of God's beneficence; he sees it rather as land that's *sorry*. And so he finds in the economic chaos of the time not simply an obscure sort of karma at work, paying America back for having overextended her dominion, but rather evidence of the direct hand of an angry and avenging God, who sees a land rich in milk and honey lying wasted by neglect. If mineral wealth is not exploited, it becomes a wasted blessing.

"Waste is a sin, America is wasteful," he intoned solemnly one spring afternoon, sitting in the Fort Worth Club and eating lobster beneath a gilt chandelier. "I'm not one of those predestinarian folks, who thinks that God just plans everything out in advance and man has no choice but to act it out. I think He sets us down and leaves us alone. When we go too far off the track, He reaches His hand in and sort of stirs the pot, and that's what's happening now. We have to develop what He has given us, use our incentive to accomplish what He wills."

In Duane McDaniel's scheme of things, the profit motive is God's instrument for fulfilling the glory of His creation. Such an interpretation may seem farfetched to an outsider, but it is not altogether uncommon in Texas. The belief that God has willed the oil business into being is no more unreasonable than the conviction that, if a man has been born lucky, he is bound to find oil.

And so Duane McDaniel—lively, full of anecdotes, yet solemn and rhetorical when he speaks seriously—searched out complicated mineral titles in Louisiana for the Moncriefs. Meanwhile, in addition to Monty Moncrief's lucky acquisition of 80,000 acres from Gulf, Dick Moncrief fell upon the sudden chance to buy a big swatch of forest right in the center of it all. "I have to take some credit for a good part of this deal," he explains. "It came from some connections I'd developed on my own."

In the course of negotiating the Israeli Deal, Dick Moncrief had become acquainted with a lot of people in the New York Jewish Community. "One day," he explained, "one of the people I had met called to tell me he was acquiring the Turner Lumber Company for twelve million dollars. He offered me the mineral leases. I looked at the map and saw the Turner was a big solid block set down in the middle of Louisiana, lots of sweetwoods and big old oaks. The guy had talked some insurance company into putting up eight and a half million for it, and he was trying to raise the rest. So I said, what the hell, we'll put up the other four million or whatever. The idea of owning all that timber appealed to me."

And so it was that the Moncriefs, on this rare occasion, invested in something other than oil or oil leases—80,000 acres of the finest forest land in America. "We cut the wood, sold it, sold off the land for farms, and kept the mineral rights," said Dick Moncrief. The deal seemed to him as if it had to be lucky, for the land he'd unexpectedly been offered lay right in the middle of the acreage his grandfather had been trying to farm out from Gulf and Phillips.

"The Gulf had sunk forty million dollars into the area," Monty Moncrief said. "But we're optimists. We wanted to gamble, and we figured we could find something everyone else had overlooked." To that end, George Bouline set up an office in Houston, and began to study every geologic conformation he could identify in Central Louisiana. Because the sand pods he sought were isolated and disparate, the seismic records which Gulf and Phillips had run on the area (and which the Moncriefs, like most independents, had to buy from the big companies) were of little use. The seismics did, however, delineate the sweep of buried coral reef, and by comparing its intricate curve across Louisiana with the way it had lain in East Texas, a model based on the Seven Oaks play was made.

From these projections, George Bouline determined where the first four-million-dollar wildcat should be drilled. That well came in unexpectedly rich and deep, and as we have seen, it yielded gas instead of oil. Rig delays had become common by that time, because of increased domestic drilling, so the Moncriefs had to wait months before commencing their second well. That one cost three million dollars, and it proved dry. A third well, just to the east of the first discovery, was described by Monty Moncrief as "another elephant—big game this time." From its depths, a few million more feet of gas were produced each day.

By this time, the Moncriefs suspected that they might

have found another Jay. Shell had drilled a rich deep well just to the east, and it seemed possible that an entire trend of fertile sands might run through the Tuscaloosa, a rich continuum deposited against the old coral reef. But it did not: Central Louisiana was not the Jay, a wide-ranging field across which one well could be drilled next to another. Each deposit of oil-bearing rock lay separately here, in a hop-scotch pattern, and some were wet and some were dry.

"We had ourselves some shoot there anyway," said Monty Moncrief, and of course that was true. But time's wheel had begun to turn, and already a shadow was being cast across the desert on the other side of the world, a shadow which looked as if it might one day grow as long as the one that Monty Moncrief had cast over Texas for so many years. The Louisiana strike proved a fitting end to his great and legendary career, and an especially appropriate one as well, for it lay in the same horizon of rock in which his first discovery had been made. But it was still an end, whereas the Israeli Deal, which Monty Moncrief had rejected smoothly a few years before with a murmured "B.L.N.T.," was only beginning.

13

Veal Chop Man

ONE HOT AFTERNOON in the late spring of 1978, when the Israeli Deal was very much on his mind, Dick Moncrief took a drive around the 17,000 acres of prime Parker County ranchland that the Moncriefs own just west of Fort Worth. Buying the land had been part of a second-generation attempt at diversification. "Ranching was Tex's idea," Monty Moncrief explained. "I'm an oilman myself." He proceeded then to compare the economics of beef unfavorably with the economics of oil, remarking upon how oil offered none of the headaches that attend having "all those little baby cows to worry about."

The ranch has nevertheless proven to be an investment which the first and the third generations can appreciate. Gas was discovered upon it in the middle '70s. "Everyone knew that there was petroleum in Parker County," Dick Moncrief explained as he drove past a small tank into which gas was being lined, a tank that glinted silver in the late-afternoon sun. "But it lies shallow, at five thousand feet." He raced through the economics of the proposition as quickly as his grandfather had run down his comparison of oil and beef. "That means when gas was seventeen cents, you could make only about ninety dollars a day, or twenty-seven hundred a month. So if a well cost fifty thousand dollars, it would take you three years before it started to pay out. Who'd drill with those kind of figures?" Dick Moncrief smiled. "But then the ceiling went up, and we brought in the rigs. Now even this land is blooming."

Still, the blooming land across which he drove could not hold his interest for very long. Heading toward the pastures where herds of Herefords grazed upon short grasses, and driving across groves planted with famous Parker County peaches, he let his thoughts wander to far-off places. He recounted all the ports of call a drill-supply ship might make when sailing from Singapore to the Gulf of Suez. He speculated upon the dangers that a stopover in Colombo might present to a transport vessel. He wondered aloud about the possibility of getting CIA support for small companies that did business with East African revolutionaries. As he spoke, he passed rows of grapevines planted in the hope of producing that much talked-about but never-realized brew, good West Texas wine. The well-tended cattle and the grape arbors husbanded by an enologist declared the land to be in a state of advanced cultivation, no longer a frontier, and frontiers were of course what interested Dick Moncrief. In search of them, he traveled to distant corners of the globe.

He brought his cream-colored Cadillac Seville to a halt at the end of a gravel path, and got out to search the horizon for evidence of a rig unreachable by the road. He had wanted to walk over and inspect it, but he abandoned the idea after opening the door to his air-cooled car and feeling the heat of the sun. He stood then in the bright wind and tangled mesquite and the sandy rough soil, wearing a dark three-button suit and a monogrammed shirt, too sharp and too carefully tailored perhaps by a shade. He looked very

much the master of all he surveyed, and he began to speak
of the deal that his family had made in Central Louisiana.

"We had a beautiful picture of the reef," he said, recalling
the seismics that delineated the arc of coral along which the
discoveries lay. His hands sketched out the shape of a limestone formation in the air; the lime had been laid down as
marine ooze by long-vanished seas. "We could see a layer of
sandstone dipping into that reef, so we drilled down to six-
teen thousand feet and hit our elephant," he said.

"We took it all," he yelled from where he was standing.
"Everything!" He walked briskly across the graveled path
and swung open the cattle guard that blocked his Cadillac's
path. The gate had been casually fastened with a rusty
horseshoe, which seemed to comment mutely upon the luck-
iness of this land.

"We took Louisiana," he shouted, holding the horseshoe
up to the light and then tossing it into the wind. "And after
that, *we took the world!*"

Dick Moncrief believed that *the world* lay open to him,
lay open to all independent oilmen with the resources and
the cunning to go international. He had looked at *the world*
and seen enough unstable zones to convince him that his
was an era uniquely suited to the making of private agreements with other countries.

A few weeks after Dick Moncrief's drive around Parker
County, when the Louisiana wells were still coming in and
oil was being drilled in the Sinai, Dick Moncrief had lunch
with his grandfather at a suburban restaurant in Fort
Worth. Lunch anywhere except at the Fort Worth Club was
unusual for the older man, but his grandson liked to try out
different places and had asked him to come along. During
the course of their lunch, Dick Moncrief explained to his
grandfather how he believed that the boundaries of the
world were the frontier that lay open to him now, whereas

his grandfather had been confined to a domestic frontier. And during the course of their lunch, the essential differences between the first and third generations were displayed at every turn in the conversation.

Dick Moncrief ordered broiled fish and a bottle of Soave Bolla, while Monty Moncrief stared over his eyeglasses at the "Continental Style" entrées listed on the menu with the ill-disguised impatience of a man who, when he wants to eat well, eats at home.

"They do a nice veal chop here, Granddad," Dick Moncrief said.

"Dickie," the older man answered, casting the menu aside in disgust, "I'm just not a veal chop man."

The difference between one who is and one who is not a *veal chop man* is the difference that defines it all. For it is the difference between a cosmopolitan generation that, even in Texas, can no longer see America as the very centerpiece of all creation, and a generation which still lives with an unquestioning sense of this country's special destiny, and the consequent inappropriateness of all things foreign. It is the difference in how one sees one's place in the world.

Monty Moncrief grew up amid the relative want and the harshness of a developing frontier land, and made hundreds of millions of dollars over the course of his eighty-odd years. He had realized his ambitions in a town that he helped to settle and shape and make grow, and so he had been able to trace his shadow, leave his mark upon an empty land, and set a standard for those who were to follow. He created a dynasty in a single special place, and he never looked at the wider world as something that concerned him particularly. "Europe?" he replied, when asked if he'd traveled there. "Yes, I've been over to Europe, during the war of course, and once or twice with Sid Richardson on one of those damn fact-finding panels that Lyndon Johnson was always dreaming up." But his travels had never suggested to Monty

Moncrief that he might with profit bring back home the
tastes and the habits of other lands. He was, after all, a man
who could explain his eighty-five years in the world by saying, "I just tried to live a clean life and do the right thing."
Such a statement might sound naïve or false to unaccus-
tomed ears, but in truth it marked him as a man of his place
and his time.

The conversation at lunch that spring day began with
Africa, for Dick Moncrief was still high from the excitement
of his success in Israel and eager to turn his eyes elsewhere
abroad. Africa, embroiled in turmoil and revolution, looked
unstable enough to favor the making of private agreements.

"I don't know if you know about Africa, Granddad," Dick
Moncrief began. "But it opens the whole world up. The majors are just not a competitive force in places like that any
more." When this news failed to elicit any response, Dick
Moncrief continued. "The situation now is just like it was in
the fifties, when the international business opened up and
the majors abandoned America to people like you. That was
your opportunity, and this is ours today."

"I can't see why you're writing off the majors, Dickie,"
Monty Moncrief replied in an impatient tone.

"It's just that it's gotten more difficult for them because
governments are falling apart so fast everywhere. And all
these new corporate regulations make it difficult for public
companies to do business with foreign governments."

Monty Moncrief took his time before replying. "Well,
Dickie, you know I have my reservations on this sort of
thing."

"It just requires a different approach, Granddad."

"Yeah, and a lot more money," said Monty Moncrief, but
again his grandson was ready. "But we've got the money,"
he said. "We've got it because you've been so successful.
The whole point is that the majors are going to have a hard
time of it because they can't deal as fast as we can."

Monty Moncrief appeared as unimpressed by this analysis

as he had been by the suggestion of the veal chop. "Don't fool yourself, Dickie. The world is still open to the majors."

"But it's hard for them, Granddad. You're dealing there with strongmen who say, 'I want a million for myself, I want a million for my country, I want to send my son to school in America . . .'"

"Well, we just don't subscribe to that way of doing business, Dickie," his grandfather answered. "We didn't get our reputation for honesty by dealing that way."

"But that's just Jaycee moralism today," Dick Moncrief replied. "Who says it's our business to go preaching ethics to the world, to tell them they should be doing things like we do them in Fort Worth? Isn't that how this country got into trouble in the first place?"

"I don't know about this country being in trouble," said the older man. "I know some of you young people think it is. But I think a man is responsible for keeping his own house in order, no matter what ranking that house has. That's what makes a reputation." But reputation is precisely what Dick Moncrief has gone abroad to escape. Of what avail might reputation be when dealing with a revolutionary government in Marxist Angola?

"I just believe that the domestic deals are still there to be made," Monty Moncrief said. "Now more than at any time in the last twenty years."

"That's true," answered Dick Moncrief, exposing the heart and true purpose of the discussion at last. "But there's nothing here that can top what you've done, Granddad."

A change in orientation—looking to the wider world rather than just to Fort Worth, while remaining in Fort Worth by choice—is the change that defines oilmen of the third generation. In being like their grandfathers, *not content,* they are nevertheless willing to recognize the element of opportunism that has always activated the frontier spirit. There are fewer heart-felt rationales, less talk about man's God-given destiny to develop and exploit the land.

There is also less provincialism. The third generation, looking to the world for its frontiers, has developed a cosmopolitan taste for the sweet life, a taste nurtured in New York and San Francisco and abroad and brought back home to take the edge off the sternness of West Texas life. Its cosmopolitanism distinguishes the third generation from the first, and helps to define who is and who is not a veal chop man. The changes that third generation taste has wrought are obvious everywhere in the oil towns of Texas.

In Fort Worth, for example, a city of millionaires, there were almost no restaurants until the middle '60s, except for a few hash houses. This was true in many Texas towns, for work was still the point of frontier life, not indulging oneself in worldly pleasures. But times have changed, and "getting in some good restaurants" is spoken of in Texas oil towns as if it were proof of a general sense of civic responsibility. Assembling art collections is also held in high regard among members of the third generation; a collector, especially one who has contributed something to a local museum, is generally spoken of with great respect, commended for an assumed selflessness and generosity. An interest in "the arts" is proof of one's worldliness, and worldliness, in Texas, is a public-spirited virtue.

The third generation style is no less flamboyant than what went before it, but its cosmopolitan emphasis makes it decidedly less narrow. And what vanishes with that narrowness is the small-town self-assurance that enables a man to believe that plain dealing and the cultivation of good character and a fine reputation is the only way to get ahead in the long run. What has disappeared from the Texan landscape is the simple faith that permits a man like Monty Moncrief to explain it all by saying that he just "tried to live a clean life and do the right thing." Such easy pieties can be developed only in isolation, and so they are not commonly held by those who have exposed themselves to the values of a wider world.

An absolute belief in the positive value of enterprise for its own sake is also lost when a wider knowledge of the world's ways is acquired. Max Banks, a red-haired wildcatter from Amarillo who once declared from the cockpit of his Cessna that there was something immoral in "letting the earth lie sorry and undeveloped like when the poor Indians had it," was decidedly not a veal chop man. He acknowledged that he might be out-of-date, proclaimed it proudly in fact. But Max Banks had always believed that *making action* was the important thing in life, and in the late 1970s, he believed it still.

Max Banks had been married all his adult life to a woman who lived in oil-camp trailers with him on many an open frontier. When she died, he married a young model from Dallas named Toni, who introduced him to the finer things of life, third-generation things, like serving cheese before dinner in the living room and traveling to Bermuda when the Panhandle winds blew too cold. But although Max Banks got to see a side of life that he had never noticed before he married Toni, a side he could have afforded but had never cared about, he never developed a taste for the "fripperies," the little touches of civilized living that the third generation brought onto the old frontier. Texas, for men of the pioneer generation, has remained a land where achievement, not refinement, is the measure of all things. From this has come their idealism.

That idealism, and the moral certainty that accompanies it, has been lost among those who look at how other people in other places do things, and who declare as a consequence the futility of trying to "preach Jaycee moralism" to Central African despots. The loss has brought a change to the Texas way of doing things, a change that is mirrored perfectly in the arc of neighborhoods that run westward in Fort Worth from the Rivercrest Country Club. Those who think in terms of *the world* are likely to adopt the manners of people who play at the very biggest tables.

Dick Moncrief has cultivated the manner of a big-stakes player. He enjoys being met with such flourishing attentions as might be accorded a visiting head of state in the best restaurants in New York and Washington, a taste for which his grandfather has little use. The habit of carrying large amounts of cash in hundreds whenever he travels is another little touch that appeals to him. He's a high roller, and he likes to show it when the occasion seems right.

Bill Houck, whom he began calling "Zvi" through the course of negotiations with Israel, likes to tease Dick Moncrief about the contrast between his sparkling peacock display and his grandfather's quiet austerity. He teases him as well about his profligate use of "Moncrief Airlines," as he calls the family's three-plane fleet. But Dick Moncrief argues that time has changed only the scale on which things are done, not the spirit.

"Hell, I don't flash any more than Granddad ever did. It's just that the level has been upped. He chased guys all over West Texas in his little plane when he needed to get hold of them. I just chase them all over the world." When a two-billion-dollar field is at stake, should a man worry if his plane has to make an extra trip or two between New York and Fort Worth? All the dazzle and the flourishings, Dick Moncrief says, are just tinsel, the required bait.

14

The Face of Texas

IN THE YEARS BETWEEN 1919, when Monty Moncrief entered the oil business back in Ponca City, and the late 1960s, when his grandson Dick followed him into it, the face of Texas had been transformed. Much of the transformation could be traced directly to the oil business, which had made the state very rich and so very open to change. In the late 1970s, when many American states and cities were operating on a deficit, Texas had a three-million-dollar surplus in its coffers, despite the fact that there were no state taxes on either individuals or on corporations. Oil wealth had made the state prosperous, and prosperity had made the state popular with Americans who were eager to make a new start in life. Texas remained the wild cutting edge of the business frontier, and so people came to Texas in increasing numbers. The population grew 25 percent in fifteen years.

The new settlers came to the cities, most notably to Houston, and to Dallas and Fort Worth. Those two very distinctive north-central Texas towns were growing together so fast that developers had begun referring to them jointly as

"the Metroplex"; a sort of in-between town—a true Anywhere, U.S.A.—had sprung up between them and it took its
graceless name, D/FW, from the large international airport
that served the two cities. Such development obscured the
differences between them, obscured the fact that Fort
Worth had always meant oil and cattle while Dallas had always meant banking and insurance. Both had large indus-
tries now—Bell Helicopter, Texas Instruments—and so life in
these cities and cities like them began to reflect a new cor-
porate-industrial reality. Texas changed from a state with a
predominantly rural population in the 1950s into a state
where most people lived in urban centers by the mid 1970s.
As people from outside the state moved in and settled in the
big cities, the patriarchal traditions of oil families and the
great inter-marrying landowning clans became less important, and less well-known.

The independent oil business, which had helped to bring
about so many of these changes, had also changed. Partly,
this was a result of the economics involved. Oil rigs cost
many times more to rent by the day. And of course wells
had to be drilled much deeper now, and in more risky
and unreliable terrain, for shallow oil had been pumped
from the ground long ago. Often old wells that had been
abandoned because old rigs could not drill any deeper
had to be reopened; their gas pressure had long since been
depleted, and costly means of carbonation were necessary if
oil was to flow. Such processes were referred to as secondary
and tertiary recovery, and they were of great importance as
the oil business moved into the 1980s. All these things made
finding oil very, very expensive. Wildcatting was no longer
something that a poor boy with a little incentive and a few
faithful backers could necessarily do. The amount of capital
required to drill a well helped to keep the oil business increasingly in the hands of those families who had made their
early fortunes in it. Who besides oil families had that kind of
money to risk?

In the years after the Second World War and into the early 1950s, men could still come from older places in America and try their hand at wildcatting, much as the first frontier oilmen had done. Some, like George Bush and Robert Mosbacher, the Houston independent who helped pave the way internationally by making plays in Indonesia, were able to prosper, and they stayed on. "I'm as much a part of Texas as anybody now," said Mosbacher, who had abandoned the comforts of a large and very social Eastern clan on the Newport yachting circuit and acted the part of family black sheep by eloping with a young girl and heading for rural Texas in the '50s. He kept his eyes open, as he says, learned the value of a handshake deal, and found that he could make Texans believe in him, trust in his luck. But adventures like his were more difficult to undertake twenty years later, in an era of rising costs.

The oil business in its late boom years was also much more tightly regulated than it had been in the early days of Ranger and the East Texas field. This was very much a result of its own success. For the abuses in the early years had inspired the men who were in it for the long run to demand the limits upon the number of wells that could be sunk into a formation in order to prevent overdrilling and waste. Ventures into the oil fields had to be licensed and approved by the Texas Railroad Commission in the oil business's modern era, and this procedure discouraged outsiders from trying their luck.

But many thousands of Americans were still intrigued by the glamour and the sense of risk that has always characterized the independent oil business, and by the promise of large profits. And so they tried their luck in the same way that some people had always tried their luck—by investing their money in promotional deals. Of course there had been promoters in the business ever since oil was discovered in America. They were men—or groups of men—who raised money to acquire leases and drill, and who kept a percent-

age of the profits from the deal even if the well came in dry.
But promoters had changed a lot in the days since Monty
Moncrief had come into the business: like many formerly
dubious entrepreneurs in America, they had gone respectable. The differences and similarities between the new promoters and the old provides a good illustration of how style
and scale in the oil business have changed, while substance
has remained remarkably the same.

American Quasar is a Fort Worth promotional company.
It is a corporation in which the public may buy stock, and it
has proven astonishingly lucrative for its early investors.
American Quasar raises money to acquire mineral leases and
to drill for oil from people who are willing to put up more
than five thousand dollars to meet exploration costs. These
participants must trust the oil-finding expertise—and the
luck—of the company's officers, and of the geologists and
landmen it employs. These men get their salaries in good
times and in lean times. The good times at American Quasar
have been many.

American Quasar has the absolutely respectable accou-
trements of any substantial American corporation—the open
books, the shareholder's statements, the investor's brochures, the large and friendly offices in a downtown bank
building. But to independents like Monty Moncrief, such
companies still amount to "just a bunch of promoters." Their
ability to raise cash from the public gives them a competitive
edge over independents, because they can indulge in speculation and because they don't have to drill and develop their
leaseholdings right away. Like all corporations, they incur a
certain amount of waste because decisions can't be made by
one man. Although he will acknowledge the enormous success that American Quasar has enjoyed, particularly in the
inaccessible and hard-to-drill Rocky Mountains, Monty
Moncrief and independents like him still refer to such companies in the same breath with the flamboyant old-style

promoters who used to hang around the old Westbrook Hotel.

Hotels like the Westbrook were a staple of the Texas oil business in its early days. They have since vanished from the scene, leaving an impression of great change, for they had provided a public space where the workings of the business, the wheeling and dealing, might be observed first hand. They were to the oil business what the New York Stock Exchange and the Chicago commodities exchange are to high finance and the business of agriculture: colorful and concrete illustrations of the liveliness of exchange, which eventually proved superfluous to the real work of trading and so became functionally obsolete. The great oil business hotels of Texas were not needed in the modern era of large cities and quick travel, but the promoters who made them flourish may still be found in different, if less colorful, guise.

Perhaps the prototype of the oil business hotel was the famous Scharbauer in Midland. Promoters and leasehounds from all over Texas visited its coffee shop to exchange leases; farmers and ranchers walked in as poor and anxious men straining under heavy mortgages and came out with their pockets bulging. Hotels like the Scharbauer were different from the temporary inns that proliferated in boomtowns and closed as soon as the rush was over. They were permanent establishments, where promoters carried on their business.

The Westbrook Hotel, together with the booster spirit of men like Amon Carter, helped establish Fort Worth as an oil town, the gateway to the riches of the West. The Westbrook was a grand-scale version of the old Ardmore domino parlor, where men once gambled for leases. The hotel stood downtown, grand and spacious in true "palace of the migrant" style; its style was a holdover from the days of the great cattleman's hotels, and its fixtures were luxurious and baroque. Around its marble mezzanine, promoters set up tables and held court. During boom years, when men rank with the smell of oil came to town with cash to buy leases, the management at the Westbrook removed the furniture from the lobby to better accommodate the frenzy of trade.

Presiding over this improvised exchange stood the cast-bronze form of a naked woman, rumored to have been smuggled from Italy and conveyed by unknown means to Fort Worth. The statue was known throughout the West as the Golden Goddess, and optimists seeking their share in the future rubbed leases on her backside before they went out to drill in the fields. This booster muse of the plains, this embodiment of the frontier spirit, stood proudly in the oil business's great early heyday, but the spirit of the frontier itself demands change, and her days of glory were destined to be brief.

During the Westbrook's last ignominious days as one of a chain of Lanvin Retirement Clubs, the marble mezzanine where millions had been made and lost was turned into a television parlor for old people, and the Golden Goddess transformed into an electrical outlet for the set. And when the old hotel was finally imploded, stuffed with dynamite and blown away from within, the Golden Goddess was "restored" and transferred to the entryway of the new Spaghetti Warehouse, formerly a meat-packing plant on the north side of town. Her history might serve as a perfect parable of frontier progress, for with very little self-consciousness, the booster spirit embalms for the amusement of tourists that which has only recently inspired optimistic dreamers. With the implosion of the old Westbrook, a reminder of an earlier era in the oil business vanished, but despite the change in style, the substance of that world of promoters and leasehounds has remained the same.

There were other things in the business that did not change much in the years since Monty Moncrief first came into it. The attitude toward private ownership of the land remained the same. The absolute right to own a piece of property—"from the core of the earth clear up to the clouds

and beyond," as one Texan described it—has remained the
basis of the independent oil business in America, the sine
qua non upon which every deal is based. Other countries do
not dispense unrestricted rights to the land, do not permit its owners and keepers to retain royalties from minerals; owners in some cases are not permitted to chop
down even a single tree. The increasing amount of land
being brought under protection by the Federal government,
particularly in the Western states, has somewhat reversed
the thoroughly American policy of earlier years, particularly
because development of minerals is usually restricted on
federal lands. But in Texas, there are very few restricted
lands—few parks or preserves, or even Indian reservations of
substantial size. On the lands which the state itself holds,
substantial development, especially of petroleum reserves,
has been encouraged. The frontier ideal of private ownership remains an article of faith among wildcatters.

Nor has the concept of the "handshake deal" been altered
with the passing of time. A traveler in the world of private
oil empires will still be told time and again that, "here in
Texas, a man's word is his bond." The code of honor that developed as a necessity in a land where lawyers and judges
were few remains an ideal and a practice in a state that now
boasts the most famous jurists in America, as well as three of
the six largest law firms. Family tradition and good-old-
boyism assure a measure of informality and trust unusual in
a more modern and regularized America, and the lessening
of opportunity for those who come from outside the business
during the last twenty years has made this practice even
more common. Larry Meeker, the Fort Worth oil family heir
who played on a modest scale, expressed it as well as anyone. "If I call Perry Bass on the phone and tell him I am
drilling a well in Mississippi, he might say, hell, boy, put me
down for an eighth. And I'd just go ahead and cut him in for
an eighth, and not wait until I got his check in the mail before I did. Now some lawyer or accountant or the Internal

Revenue Service might tell me that's not how you do business. I'd just tell him, my friend, you do it your way, and we'll do it our way down here. It seems to have worked pretty well for us."

Although it takes more money to wildcat now than it once did, and although the stakes are higher, the science of oil-finding hasn't made the enterprise a safe bet, and the old element of risk remains. The science has given oilmen such tools as seismic maps, but these are of use only when oil lies buried in large structural traps, along anticlines. When oil lies in stratographic formations—along shoreline faults or in sandbars—seismics cannot help detect its presence. The likelihood of finding a rank wildcat is still about one chance in ten, and luck remains the prerequisite for success.

Nor has the clannishness that prevails among the wealthier long-time residents of Texas changed much. It was born out of a real physical isolation from the rest of the country and a sense of shared hardship, but even though these things no longer exist, a certain remove from the mainstream of American life has continued to characterize life in the state. The distinctive institutions of Texas—the local petroleum clubs, the very active chapters of the Junior League, the cotillions, even the Neiman-Marcus department stores—have combined to make a distinctive way of life, a common experience, that defines the clannishness of the old families in the state made rich by oil and by land.

The network of friends and relatives that most families maintain within the state contributes to the clan feeling as well. It would not be common to find a New York City heiress who spent lots of time in Rochester, Albany, and Buffalo each year, but a Fort Worth heiress might visit Dallas, Austin, and Houston every month; she might have lived briefly in these cities, and she would almost certainly have a defined and regular social circle in all of them. The outsider in Texas will notice immediately how much people move around within the state. Travel between the larger cities is brisk, and facilitated by an airline that flies only within the state, at frequent intervals and at very low prices, often making use of the older terminals that were abandoned when the new international airports were built. The ease of frequent air travel has indeed spread the habit of hopping around within the state among those who are not rich themselves, and so it further defines and characterizes life in the state of Texas.

And so we see how the face of Texas has changed in the years since Monty Moncrief first came into the oil fields. These changes have affected the oil business in many easily discernible ways, but they have not changed its substance, its basic themes. The element of risk, the importance of private ownership with few restrictions, the competition from promoters, the uncertain technology, the persistent clannishness—these things had characterized the business from the start, and they continued to define it still. The third generation had inherited a complex tradition, and it would work within this tradition even when it took its business to far off lands.

15

Romance and Rebellion

IN DICK MONCRIEF'S OFFICE, there hangs a single photograph. It shows his father, Tex, wearing his customary scowl. Beneath it is written simply, "Count Me Out!" "Tex is a pessimist," Monty Moncrief once observed about his son. "And Dickie's an optimist. I'm an optimist myself, of course."

The distinction is characteristic of that between the three generations in Texas. Optimism has become the mode of youthful rebellion. Max Banks, the drilling contractor from the desolate Panhandle whose age marks him as second-generation but whose spirit and independence (he began life as a roustabout) classify him with the first, defined Texas-style optimism. "Optimism," he said, "is what has made the West a land of builders, instead of a land of adders-on. Maybe I'm out-of-date," he sighed mournfully one afternoon as he piloted his twin-engine Cessna over the vast expanse of half-million-acre cattle ranches, which are the rule upon the high plains, "but I believe building and growing and making action is what America is all about. Improving the land, instead of letting the earth lie sorry and undeveloped like when the poor Indians had it."

Indians, in whatever guise, are still the enemy in the West. They symbolize to the frontier booster a passive spirit that bows before nature rather than seeking to conquer it. Regulators play the role of Indians in this scheme of things, as do pessimists and doubters. The second generation spirit goes against that earlier one, which settled this harsh and willful land. "Count me out" is not a motto that could have won the West. Optimism, the desire to expand and build, is a third-generation rebellion against it, one that perfectly assimilates the Texas tradition of the grandfather-hero.

Dick Moncrief was born the third of Tex Moncrief's six children. Tex divorced his first wife after Dick Moncrief was born and married Deborah Beggs, the daughter of a North Texas ranching family famous for beautiful blond daughters who allied the Beggses with the great oil and cattle families of Texas. Deborah had been married to a doctor, with whom she had two children, and the children of both Tex and Deborah's first families grew up along with those children they had together. There were eight of them in all.

Tex's second family inherited the Beggs family's fair complexions and freckles. Dick Moncrief inherited his grandfather's good looks. He is tall, dark, and well-made, with the peculiar long earlobes that run like a birthmark among Texas oil and cattlemen. He has the natural robustness and unselfconscious good health so characteristic of this part of America that it appears almost as if the principle of natural selection has been at work. And he dresses sharp, like his grandfather—his tailoring is always perfect, and his shirts are monogrammed white-on-white. There is something about him that is a bit flashy, but never in bad taste. And there is also something a shade too careful about his manner at times, less spontaneous than his grandfather's, less trusting of his own instinct. Still, in Texas, when a man puts everything together right, they say with characteristic understatement that "his pants fit him," and Dick Moncrief's pants fit him fine.

The large family Tex Moncrief raised spent its younger years in a modest suburban neighborhood on the west side of Fort Worth, a few blocks from Monty Moncrief's house and the Rivercrest Country Club. Only later did they move into the second-generation Crestline neighborhood on the other side of the golf course. Along with the fierce fighting and the fierce loyalty, a certain air of misfortune hung over the family, an ironic counterpoint to the good fortune of its inheritance. The oldest son is rarely mentioned outside the family, and is not a visible part of the family business; the second son, Herbie, was killed in a motorcycle crash before his chance to prove himself came; the youngest child and only daughter died of leukemia in childhood.

It has been observed that large families of boys, some of whom die young in freakish and terrible ways while others fail obscurely and are rarely spoken of, are something of a rule in Texas cities like Fort Worth. The daughter of a North Texas German cattle baron, who has watched these strange tragedies through the years and can give detailed accounts of them, maintains that they occur with such uncanny frequency here because the coil of family is wound so tightly it cannot survive without some breaking of the springs, and because the polarity of impossibly tough men and impossibly sweet women that exists in Texas is too extreme to achieve a sane balance. The repressed rage of women bred to be strong but then sheltered like children and kept idle must sometimes find in cataclysms its hysterical, indirectly murderous vent.

All along the curve of Crestline, evidence of this tension can be observed. "Stinky Davis was as tough as he had to be to live up to his name," said an old oilman who lived down the block from Monty Moncrief. "But Miss Alice was one of our finest ladies." Stinky and Miss Alice were the parents of the ill-starred Davis boys, who fought and sued and chopped up an oil equipment empire between them before Cullen, the middle son, was arrested and tried for a celebrated shotgun murder spree. The Davises give instance of the negative energy of this familiar family constellation, but the Moncriefs' positive energies are charged with the dynamism of these same conflicts. Tex is a hard man and Deborah is a soft woman, and money never made their lives run smoothly.

Tex Moncrief is gruff and somewhat plain, a man of few words. He lives in a world defined by plane trips to remote well sites and daily log reports, golf games played under a hot sun, and the ceaseless masculine companionship of his father and his sons. He speaks of work as the only justification for human existence. "Of course they went on business," he snapped when asked about a trip to Scotland and Italy that his sons Charlie and Tom Oil Moncrief had taken. They'd recounted their adventures with a relishing emphasis on night life and high-spirited drinking bouts, but Tex would have none of that. "*Of course* it was business," he said. "Everything we Moncriefs do is business." Deborah Moncrief, pliable, round, and soft as a dove, is talkative and blond and jeweled, Tex's opposite. She lives in a world defined by a family now grown and the flowers she tends with unceasing care. After fifty years on earth, she is a woman still willing to be told where to stand and where to sit; she seeks justification in her willingness to serve and her kindness. Tex and Deborah demonstrate as perfectly as any pair in Texas the polarity between men and women of which the German cattle heiress spoke, and the gift for tragedy as well. But whatever its sources, tragedy binds, and in Texas, families are bound.

Within the parameters of these tensions and this drama, Dick Moncrief always did what was expected of him. He went to prep school at an Indiana military academy, like many another oilman's son. Then he entered the University of Texas at Austin to study petroleum engineering. When he

graduated in the middle 1960s, he did what was not expected: he refused to join his father and his grandfather, or
to take an apprenticeship in Midland or Hobbs, New Mexico, before returning to work in the office in Fort Worth.
Dick Moncrief knew he wanted something different, something he thought his hometown could never offer him.

And so he went to New York City, where he took a man-
agement-training job at an old and very Jewish investment
company. This was a shocking move back home in Fort
Worth. "What I did was heresy," Dick Moncrief recalls, "a
scandal, a terrible slap in the face, as bad as anything someone in my family could do." And while joining the ranks of a
venerable banking house may not be everyone's idea of the
extreme among mid-1960s youthful rebellion, one must always consider the context. In Texas, in the oil business, the
future is not a matter left open to choice, something for each
child to determine in the modern American way. In Texas,
family is destiny.

"Granddad did it all in America," Dick Moncrief always
says, and when he was younger, he believed that the only
way he could escape the older man's shadow and leave a
mark of his own on the world was to leave Texas and the oil
business behind him. But of course the desire to put distance between himself and what was familiar, the reluc-
tance to accept what was his by fortune and merely act as
guardian over that, was in fact exactly what linked him to
the man who regarded his departure as heretical—his grandfather. His was the same old hankering after the unknown
that had driven men West one hundred years before, away
from the civilized world and onto the empty plains where
virgin grasses grew.

For Dick Moncrief, going to New York City in the mid-
1960s was the pioneering thing to do. Those were precisely
the years during which the independent oil business appeared to offer little of interest to anyone in whom the frontier spirit—"romance," as it's called among oilmen—was still

alive. The opportunity to be anything more than a guardian looked as if it did not exist; the Jay field, which would herald and presage the boom, had not yet been struck, and gas was not worth producing. The known reserves of new oil—in the Panhandle and across the Rocky Mountain belt—lay too deep for drilling when the price of oil remained below three dollars a barrel. This would all change after 1973, of course, but that change lay far in the future when Dick Moncrief went to New York City.

He chose to live in the grand, high-rising, and elegant Essex House Hotel on Central Park South, where another hometown boy had also taken up residence. But even having a compatriot with whom to share such magnificent quarters did not alleviate the loneliness of life in a city where Dick Moncrief found that anonymity need not be sought, but rather escaped from. His was a loneliness shared by many who come from close-knit down-home towns in the South. Money is no palliative for it.

He speaks of his year in New York as one of confusion. Much of it seems to have focused on women, and while this might seem surprising in the case of a young man so wonderfully rich and handsome and young who kept rooms at the Essex House Hotel, it must be remembered that Dick Moncrief came from a world where women were considered a breed apart, creatures in need of protection and aid. He'd passed his younger years in a military academy, and had attended college at a school to which debutantes still transfer during their sophomore year so they can be home to prepare for the ritual festivities. He emerged from this with a perfect Southern chivalry intact, a chivalry at ease and appropriate in Texas, but a chivalry that may have been lost upon the girls from here and there he found himself dating up North. He recalls with odd insistence the tales he heard from women in New York of their abuse at the hands of Northern men and their gratitude for his gallant protection. Such recollections formed his chief impression of the city as a place almost too tough for the innocent to survive in. Nor did he discover himself particularly suited to the step-by-step climb up the corporate ladder, a slow and controlled series of moves inimicable to the Texas free-form style. The feeling that he was in alien territory began to grow upon him.

The pull of the old hometown seems to exert itself more strongly upon Texans than upon those who have come from somewhere else. Midwesterners, for example, who leave home to live for a while on the East Coast or in Europe, do not often return to Oshkosh after exploring the wider world. But in even the smallest backcountry Texas towns, one meets people who have moved back home after time spent abroad and made their peace with that. They are exceptions every one of them to the standard American pattern of moving up by moving on.

Perhaps it's because of the blood. Or perhaps it's because the men and women who settled this harsh land had to work so hard to make a living that they make it proportionately hard on children who try to leave behind birthrights so toilsomely won. Or maybe it's just that Texans, who travel in packs, surrounded by family and friends whose families they know, feel isolated when they aren't in the company of others like themselves. Whatever the reason, Dick Moncrief felt the pull, and though life at the Essex House Hotel had its sweetness, one year in New York was enough.

He did not figure his decision to leave as a defeat, however. For he had conceived of a scheme, at once bold and familiar, whereby he might make peace with his hometown on his own terms. He would continue to seek the anonymity and independence he had looked for in New York by taking his own family's business abroad. "I realized that I would like to stay in Fort Worth if I could get something international, even though my family thought that was crazy," he said. "So I made those my terms for going back."

There was no sign at the time of the boom that would soon bring the sons and grandsons of oilmen back home to

Texas from further afield than New York. Domestic prospects for expansion still looked bad. But the chances for an independent operating successfully abroad looked even worse. This had always been true.

Wildcatter wisdom had gone against foreign deals ever since the early days, when Glenn McCarthy, once the toughest, meanest, richest, and most flamboyant of the Texas wildcatters, lost his fortune in the treacherous inland swamps of Colombia. And it was a tradition that continued still, having been proven once more in the early 1970s, when Bunker Hunt saw his billion-dollar concession to Libya's sands slip away from him at the stroke of General Qaddafi's pen. Independents had simply never had the power to hold their own against the governments of entire countries. Even trying to find oil internationally was considered a foolish gesture by those who were in the business for the long run, like Monty Moncrief.

16

The Sweet Life

DICK MONCRIEF'S FIRST MOVE was considerably less bold than Glenn McCarthy's or Bunker Hunt's had been, although his subsequent ventures would not prove so.

He had been traveling in Italy, along the Amalfitano coast, when he chanced to hear that the Italian national oil company was sponsoring an auction for the rights to drill along the shores of Sicily. Gulf Oil was one of the bidders, and because Monty Moncrief had for years nurtured a special relationship with Gulf down in Houston, trading acreage with the company and sharing geologic speculation, Dick Moncrief knew about the auction. News of it presented him with his first opportunity to acquire oil property abroad, and so he went against the advice of his family and gambled some money on a percentage of Gulf's deal. The first hole they drilled cost ten million dollars. It proved dry.

"I was a bachelor then," Dick Moncrief says now of his plans for drilling in Sicily, meaning that the undertaking had more to do with his desire to spend summers in Positano than with any prudent consideration of prospective geology.

Soon after this venture, he would cross paths with the man who would circle the globe for him, plucking up properties and providing everything he needed to establish himself internationally at last. But at the time he did what any hometown boy would do, and brought in a friend who knew as little about drilling for oil in Italy as he did.

His friend was a big shambling Saint Bernard of a man, the son of a Viennese musician who had ended his days in the red-dirt Baptist town of Abilene. The son had come into the business by marrying a real-life oil princess, the ranch-bred daughter of a famous Fort Worth family. She had lived after finishing school at the Plaza Hotel in New York, and had driven her own candy-red Mercedes-Benz around the city on sunny afternoons. But the loneliness had gotten to her as it had to Dick Moncrief, and after a year, she'd come home like a good West Texas girl and done what she'd been raised up to do. She'd married the boy from Abilene, and brought him into her family's business.

The young couple moved after their marriage to the walled desert city of Midland. Being born into their world brought burdens attendant upon its blessings, chief among them an obligation to put in time doing things the hard way. For no amount of wealth can relieve the tedium or physical hardship of life in an isolated village swept by the grit of unending sandstorms. Midland is where the younger generation is sent, less as a test of their talent than of their toughness. It is a way station where they prove their devotion to the Puritan faith, not by adhering to a rigid set of principles or a code of conduct, but rather by subordinating the pleasure of the moment to the promise of the future. Like all good Puritans, young heirs of the third generation are taught to put duty before the pursuit of the sweet life.

A sense of iron-bound dutifulness, however, comes harder to those who have lived while young in the Plaza Hotel and driven candy-red Mercedes-Benzes around Manhattan. But it is a sense that nevertheless may still be acquired in Texas,

where young people come back home and do what they've
been bred up to do.

The oil princess loved the walled gardens of Midland,
which made it seem an oasis or a desert mirage. She and her
husband made the best of their circumstances there. But
when Dick Moncrief presented them with the opportunity
of doing business while living in Rome's Hassler-Villa Me-
dici Hotel, it was an offer they couldn't refuse. The better
part of a year was spent—some back home might have said
lost—on the Sicilian venture, which yielded no profits and
cost a few million. But it taught them something of the
sweet life that they could have learned only in a land where
pleasures are not routinely deferred. They brought back a
taste for that sweetness. And although they would never
abandon stern duty, neither would they ever forget that
they had known something else.

It is this fond nostalgia for sweet things and beauty that
softens the third generation and distinguishes it from the
first, that sets Dick Moncrief apart from his grandfather.
The young wife of his partner from Abilene left the Via
Veneto for Midland with the high spirits and good grace
characteristic of her kind. But the sight of artichokes piled
high upon the shelves of a shopping center supermarket
back home brought tears to her eyes one day when she saw
it, for she had eaten artichokes—tender little ones, as she
recalled—in Italy every day. And she wondered for a moment, seeing them again, why she, who could have lived
anywhere in the world, had chosen exile in this desolate
corner of it, so far from any spirit of sweetness. The answer
to her question was of course in her blood.

After the ill-fated Sicilian venture, her husband abandoned his attempt to expand the family fortunes in such
novel ways, or to conquer frontiers of which those who had
come before him had never dreamed. He turned his attention once more to the Permian red beds along which the oil
fields of West Texas lie. But Dick Moncrief always thought

in terms of frontiers and expansion, and he saw in this first failure proof that it was at least possible for him to go abroad and conduct his family business on his own terms. Upon returning home for good, he married a girl named Marsland Buck from an established but not especially wealthy Fort Worth family with landholdings west of town. They were married within six weeks of their deciding.

She was scarcely more than twenty at the time, but she knew exactly what she wanted. A woman who watched them both grow up said, "Marsland had set her cap for Dickie long beforehand, and she stuck it out until she got him. She just made up her mind that she had to have that boy." She is a small dark girl with frail delicate beauty, who looks like a teenager as she enters her thirties, but Dick Moncrief, when he speaks of her, mentions always her toughness, her determination, and her unshakable self-respect. He is sure that she would leave him if he stepped out of line, without a backward glance at the money or all the things that go with being a Moncrief. It was just this toughness of course that won him, that brought him down, as he says, at the age of twenty-nine.

After their marriage, they bought and moved into the cool white limestone Spanish-style villa where the great ranch heiress of North Texas, Anne Valiant Burnett Waggoner Winfour Hall Tandy, had lived with one of the string of husbands who had died before her. She left that house's shady loveliness for a spare stone-and-glass geometric structure built for her by I. M. Pei a few blocks to the west, the better to house her collection of Braques, Picassos, and Modiglianis. After the old villa stood empty for a while, Dick Moncrief and Marsland moved in. "I thought, what the hell, if I'm going to come back home, I might as well come back in style," he says, explaining his decision to purchase while still so young this particular stately extravagance, still referred to locally as "Anne Tandy's old house." The villa, set amid groves of glossy live oaks and thick-leaved magnolias, and

mirrored in a shaded swimming pool that runs alongside a
low-roofed pavilion opposite, is hidden at the end of a curving drive that runs through the west side of town. Its set-
ting, of course, perfectly illustrates Dick Moncrief's place at
the far end of the generational arc that cuts across Fort
Worth's oil-rich neighborhoods.

Upon moving into their house, Dick Moncrief and his
wife undertook to completely redesign its already elaborate
and tasteful rooms. This has proven an unending task, which
has consumed their time through the years, keeping them
tied to Fort Worth far more than they had planned, circum-
scribing their social life, limiting their chances to entertain,
and turning their lives upside down. But Dick Moncrief always speaks of the task as a responsibility, a duty that could
not be escaped.

His lament is a familiar one in Texas, where major redecorating schemes are commonplace, where Norman cha-
teaus are transformed into Renaissance palaces, Colonial
mansions into geometric open spaces, and medieval castles
into Victorian cream puffs all the time. Their owners also
speak of such transformations as being done in the service of
duty. In this frontier land, where people seek justification
through work and put up hurdles to delay their own pleasure like atavistic pioneers, work must be made when there is
none to do.

The highest accolades a young bride can win come when
she labors to refurbish an old home, or oversees the elaborate decoration of a new one, exhausting herself in the process. In Texas, where being esteemed a "go and do" person is
desired above all, women finding themselves with very little
to actually go and do, turn the running of their homes into a
task of monumental complexity. The Puritan spirit of Midland is alive everywhere in the elaborate, time-consuming,
overdone homes of the Western plains. It is a spirit of stern
duty that finds a way to survive amid the display of riches
that might otherwise seduce those who live among them to
simply savor the pleasures of the sweet life.

17

The World

THE WORLD has always been Dick Moncrief's frame of reference, the field of his ambitions. His challenge to the limits of Texas tradition is mounted plainly on a wall in his office. Most Texas oilmen display maps on their walls— topographic or mineral distribution maps, raised reliefs embossed with the Lone Star insignia, section maps of Western counties upon which plastic tacks indicate prospective oil zones or mark recent strikes. Such maps are always of Texas, and often of Oklahoma as well, and they portray allegiance as much as they convey information.

Dick Moncrief's map, however, which stretches across an entire wall of his office, marks neither of these states. Its western cut-off point lies somewhere to the east of them, along the Louisiana Gulf Coast. The map is centered around the Mediterranean basin, and the tacks representing oil fields that are affixed to it do not mark locations along the lip of the Permian basin or the llano uplift sweep of the panhandle Anadarko, but rather delineate Middle Eastern deserts, the eastern coast of Africa, the curl of the Malaysian peninsula. Nothing illustrates so well as this map, which includes Cabinda and Sri Lanka but not the city of Fort Worth, the scope of third generation concerns.

After the ten-million-dollar dry hole in Sicily, after the decision to leave New York and come back into the family business on his own terms, after the sudden marriage with which he celebrated his return, Dick Moncrief began to look for oil properties abroad.

People who knew said it was a bad time to do it. Revolution and nationalism were sweeping the globe in the late 1960s, and governments that had signed agreements to share the production of their sands with oil companies lost power themselves in sudden coups. Overnight, firm agreements meant nothing. It was a time of confusion and pessimism, but Dick Moncrief remained a frontier optimist and refused to believe that bad times could be bad for him.

Instead, he discerned in world instability an opportunity to move in where the big oil companies were staging strategic retreats. He reasoned that it would grow increasingly difficult for the majors to operate in parts of the world where governments might lose power in the space of a week. They were accustomed to long-range plans, rather than dealing on the wing, and unsettled conditions discouraged them. Dick Moncrief figured that an independent could move more quickly, could, as he said, "drill like hell" until a government was overthrown, and then turn around and make a deal with the new regime. Since independents couldn't afford to deal in politics, to interfere with a nation's internal debates, independents could perhaps avoid exciting the resentment that made it so difficult for the majors when they were caught in a drama of coup and countercoup. And so it was that he decided to pursue instability as it quaked its path around the globe.

Dick Moncrief's plan to maneuver along frontiers where political borders were shifting met only one impediment. He didn't know enough about the international scene to be able to identify where such shifts might be likely to occur. Nothing in his schooling as a petroleum engineer or his experience as a management trainee in New York had prepared him for such decisions. And nothing in his family background gave him perspective. His grandfather was fond of proclaiming that an oilman's place was in America, and doing so in a tone that left little room for argument, especially from one who had demonstrated his expertise by participating in a ten-million-dollar dry hole in Sicily. Dick Moncrief needed an education. And perhaps even more, he needed an ally, an older man whose support might prove a counterweight to the influence of his grandfather, a neutralizing force and even a refuge.

He found what he needed in Bill Houck. As has been observed, it is not uncommon, in even the smallest of Texas towns, to meet with people who have lived for a time in London or Paris, but who have returned home and made their peace with that, people who combine a wide-ranging cosmopolitanism with the unchanging values and true interests of down home. This phenomenon is frequent among the legions of international businessmen who routinely commute between far-flung capitals of international commerce and the small towns of Texas, and whose country manner gives no hint of their savvy, their world-encompassing expertise. The surprised outsider may discover that the man drinking iced tea in the lounge of the local petroleum club and discussing the planting of pear and pecan trees on his ranch has in fact spent the past week with an ambassador in Sri Lanka and is planning to fly the following Monday to Abu Dhabi to consult with the ruling family there. Such a man will recount his itinerary with noticeable smoothness and no trace of ostentation, for such journeys are unremarkable in his life. Bill Houck is such a man.

He is a lawyer from the rolling red-dirt farm country of Western Oklahoma. His speech retains the comforting cadences of a wise country judge, while his intelligence and cool demeanor have taken him to the far ends of the earth. He negotiated the North Sea contracts between the nations that drilled for oil there, and lived in The Hague for six years while doing so. He "opened up Africa," as Dick Moncrief says, for Union Carbide during the 1960s, buying mineral concessions from governments of countries in every stage of revolution. Finally, he was hired as an international legal advisor by the Champlin Oil Company in Fort Worth. He found himself very much at home in that town, for he had remained an Oklahoma family man through all his travels.

While Bill Houck was at Champlin, he began to have lunch regularly with Dick Moncrief, who had just returned to the fold of his family and was determined to move his share in their business onto the world stage. Houck's smooth discreet bearing gives little hint of the loquacity of which he is capable when warmed to a subject that falls within his realm of expertise—Kissinger's disengagement policy in the Sinai, for example, or the complexities of Saudi Arabia's ties to Egypt. He was willing to talk, and Dick Moncrief was willing to listen, and over their lunches an alliance was formed. He decided to leave Champlin Oil. And within a week, Bill Houck found himself scouting oil properties for Dick Moncrief on the other side of the globe. "I spent twenty-seven years in corporate," he reflected, "but it just never took with me."

Houck is commandingly handsome, tall, gray-haired, and aquiline. He is dignified and perspicacious, and his manner plays well against Dick Moncrief's enthusiastic and engaging foxiness. Together they share a certain style, a perfect dark tailoring and sharpness around the cuffs that's more international than Texas: cutter-heeled boots and Lone Star tie-clasps are unimaginable here. Bill Houck's office spreads out across the second floor of the three-story Moncrief building, trim, elegant, and spare, strewn with copies of *Foreign Affairs* and the Jerusalem *Post*. It suggests the anonymousness of an international businessman, as does the office of Dick Moncrief, which is also trimmed down, modern, and cold, distinguished only by the big map of the world that spreads across one wall.

Both offices are of course entirely different from the grand old cattleman's comfort of Monty Moncrief's lair, and it is in such subtle ways that the terms of alliance have been drawn and declared. And indeed, Bill Houck is the perfect outsider-ally in this particular family drama. His experience, solidity, and basic country sense equip him well for the partisan elder's role, while a certain neat lawyerliness and the youthfulness of early middle age prevent him from cutting the truly Olympian figure that might challenge Monty Moncrief's grandeur.

Together, Dick Moncrief and Bill Houck formed Moncrief International. The company made its first forays into Indonesia, for a Houston independent had blazed the way there by acquiring some mineral leases to that country at auction, and Bill Houck had some familiarity with the old Sukarno regime. But they also turned their interest to Angola, which was then in the midst of both a colonial war for independence from Portugal and a civil war between the guerrilla factions that hoped to rule once independence had been achieved. As such, Angola seemed the right place for Dick Moncrief to test out his theories about world instability affording the right opportunity for independents. Indonesia would in fact prove a relatively stable and safe testing ground for the newly international independent, but Africa would supply its share of the cloak-and-dagger intrigue that Dick Moncrief soon discovered characterized the business he had chosen.

He had wanted to look for oil in Africa even before Bill Houck had come to work for him. That continent's frequent political shifts during the 1960s had made it increasingly unattractive to major companies, despite its mineral richness. The spread of chaos and confusion, the changing of borders, and the forming of entire new states, brought a succession of new regimes that confiscated old business contracts and sold them off to the highest bidder. The climate was hardly one to encourage investment by companies that must answer to stockholders, but it did look as if it might hold promise for an independent, a fast mover who didn't have to answer to anyone and had a taste for the frontier.

Dick Moncrief had demonstrated that taste during the days when he was still bouncing around Europe. He had flown from there secretly and alone to the drought-ravaged provincial capital of a West African country then in chaos, and had found in a government abstractor's office, lying forgotten under finger-thick layers of dust, whole drawers full of yellowing oil prospecting maps, the mother-lode key to the country. Included among them were sheaves of seismic records, which gave a picture of the fault and thrust of the inner African earth, suggesting where oil and gas might lie along upfolded anticlines.

Such treasures were fruits of the labor of men who had held concessions to this fertile land and the seas that lap its borders, but who lost their rights in the dawn surprise of sudden revolution. Dick Moncrief understood their value, but could not figure a way to make use of them. He was isolated and alone in a dusty African town, without contacts or information, much as his grandfather had once been at the Gregg Hotel back in Longview, Texas.

He left the bewildering land and returned to London, where he had been staying. From there he made the journey back to Fort Worth. He had no idea of how he might use his experience, but his interest in doing business in Africa had been stirred. When he joined forces with Bill Houck, he finally had information to put into the service of his desire.

Bill Houck and Dick Moncrief conceived of an African plan as soon as they got together. They wanted to make their first mark upon the world scene by acquiring concessions in that part of Angola that would soon be known as

Cabinda. Gulf held the offshore rights to thàt oil-rich province, but Bill Houck knew that the sands that underlay the
earth's surface there were still available because of the confusion that reigned throughout the country. He had spent a
good part of his working life in Africa, and so understood
the nature of the confusion, and he believed, as Dick Moncrief did, that they might be able to use it to their advantage. Shortly after he resigned from Champlin, he and Dick
Moncrief flew to Portugal, where the mineral rights to terri-
tories were still being administered.

"No sooner did we get there than the revolution in Portugal broke out," Dick Moncrief recalled. "Everything in
Africa changed overnight with that, and so I said to myself,
welcome to the real world. It was quite a welcome. I sat up
in my hotel room and watched it all happen." This was to be
the first in a series of baptisms by fire, in which he would
learn at firsthand the hazards of doing business where instability defined the frontier.

An interim government had been appointed to rule Angola. Bill Houck was dispatched from Portugal to Luanda,
the capital city there, so that he might negotiate directly
with the ruler, whose authority was uncertain in any case.
"The whole city was broken up, ruled over by fighting factions," Bill Houck recalled. "There were old-line Marxists,
Cubans, boys from the CIA. It was hard knowing who was
who, and you had to get a pass to get from one part of town
to another. It was a typical African situation—planes strafing
overhead while you're trying to get the minister or whoever to ignore what's happening and sign a contract with
you." When he finally got an agreement, as he recalls, he
and the President were lying under the table, and the bul-
lets were flying.

Such dedicated measures, however, proved of little avail
in Africa. The major companies had learned this through the
1960s, and now Dick Moncrief was learning it to his cost.
Within a month of having made the Cabinda deal, the gov-

ernment had changed. The minister with whom the contract had been signed was underground or in jail—nobody
was certain which.

"It was back to the bush," said Bill Houck.

18

A Trunkload of Maps

THE ANGOLAS of the world, with their predictable pattern of revolution and civil war, were something Bill Houck had seen before and would see again. But the Israeli Deal was like nothing else. So when the chance came for the newly formed Moncrief International to make what Dick Moncrief called "the greatest deal in the world" on those far away sands, everything else—Asia, Africa, big deals and small—was forgotten.

Israel had been trying to develop a reliable source of oil since it first became a state. To that end, the Israeli government had undertaken an aggressive, and ultimately disastrous, courtship of black Africa during the 1960s. Israel promised development aid in exchange for the chance to acquire oil concessions in return. By such an exchange, the country hoped to forge an alliance that would give it leverage against the Arabs, while providing itself with a source of oil.

Simple trade agreements were not what the Israelis had in mind, however. They wanted direct control over their supplies. To that end, the Israeli National Oil Company was set up to explore for and produce oil directly in such countries as Madagascar, Ethiopia, Uganda, Kenya, Ghana, and Gabon. Israel's scheme proved poorly timed, however. The star of Islam was already rising above the desert, and an alliance of Arab nations had decided to use its increasing petroleum wealth to isolate Israel from the rest of the world.

By offering aid far greater than anything Israel could have promised, the Arabs persuaded the leaders of Africa to break their contracts and reconsider the wisdom of their opposition to Moslems, whom they suspected and feared by tradition. This policy coincided with the Arab boycott of any company that did business with Israel, and soon it became impossible for the Israelis to hire a rig or contract a drill ship or even rent equipment to log their wells, so that they might continue to work in those few countries that still honored their contracts. The African policy proved disastrous, as would most of Israel's adventures in the oil trade.

During the decade he spent negotiating contracts across Africa, Bill Houck's path often crossed that of the Israeli National Oil Company. Later, he would discern in these encounters a prophetic foreshadowing of the role the company came to play in his own life. Because the Israelis were frequently his competitors for contracts, Bill Houck came firsthand by his knowledge of their complex and desperate search for oil.

He had, moreover, occasion to also learn of the mysterious drilling rig that the Israelis managed to sneak through international waters onto their own shores. It was an American rig, originally leased by Tenneco, from back home in Tulsa, and it had been shipwrecked in a Middle Eastern storm and lain washed up on the shores of Oman for two years. A Dutch salvage ship hauled it at last to Singapore for repairs, and it was being shipped from there to Malta when it suddenly lost its tow and disappeared near the Sinai Bedouin settlement of At-Tūr.

Bill Houck knew of the rig's journeyings because he had been negotiating with Tenneco when that company owned it. He did not know, of course, that the rig had "disappeared" near the Sinai by prior arrangement instead of by mere chance. The Israelis, having failed in their scheme to drill for oil in Africa, were preparing to explore the sands of the Sinai desert, which they had occupied since 1967. Their scheme was secret, of course, and Bill Houck would hear no more about the vanished rig until the day came for him and Dick Moncrief to take control of its operation.

Israel's plans for drilling in the Sinai looked jinxed from the start. Israel had taken possession of the land in the Six-Day War against Egypt in 1967, and as is customary, they had laid claim to its mineral rights during occupation. The mirror image of the Sinai had been developed on the Egyptian side into rich oil fields, and because the same geological forces had formed the sands that underlay the entire Gulf basin, the Israelis hoped that with the capture of this land they might become Middle Eastern oil producers at last.

The oil ministry in Jerusalem was given jurisdiction over the territory's petroleum wealth. Because the Israeli National Oil Company was still entangled in its ill-fated policy of African acquisition, and because no other oil company in the world was willing to anger the Arabs by exploring occupied land, the ministry granted some Sinai development rights to an American promoter named John King.

Promoters differ from independent oilmen in that they will accept funds from people with no ties to the oil business, and because they construct deals that enable them to take a cut from their investors even when the wells they drill prove dry. John King's company, King Resources, raised huge sums of money from American Jews moved by reason of patriotism or emotion to drill for oil in Israel. He took elaborate measures of underground sound waves and

drew up seismographic maps in order to determine just
where oil in the Sinai might lie. His groundwork was extensive, and it was expensive.

But King Resources never made any wells, never came
close to finding oil, although the company did manage to
spend a lot of money. During the early phases of exploration, King Resources went into receivership; John King had
been an associate of Bernard Cornfeld, and when the great
Overseas Investors scandal rocked the international financial
world, John King discovered that his days as a Middle East
high roller were over.

After King Resources went bankrupt, the search for oil in
the Sinai was suspended. It was then, as Dick Moncrief recalls, that a chance conversation between a Jewish industrialist from Fort Worth and an Israeli wheeler-dealer set the
course from which everything would follow. Lou Barnett,
the industrialist, and David Sofer, the wheeler-dealer, were
driving around Jerusalem one day, discussing their mutual
investments in Israel, when the conversation turned to a discussion of the King Resources disaster.

Dick Moncrief says it was Sofer who first mentioned that
the extensive seismics the company had made were now in
the hands of the Israeli government, floating around to not
much purpose. Barnett considered that this information
could probably be put to good use back home in Texas, for
in Texas they know how to *go and do*. And so it was, Dick
Moncrief says, that "Lou came back to Fort Worth with a
whole trunkload of geology. He just set it down and said,
'Boys, take a look at this.'"

Barnett showed the maps first to Howard Walsh, the Fort
Worth boy who had been Dick Moncrief's roommate at the
Essex House in New York; he had come back home after his
adventures there and joined his father in the oil business.
"So Howard brought the information to me," Dick Moncrief
says, "because I was the only international independent he
knew." His claim to being international, of course, rested

rather lightly at the time upon his abortive Sicilian venture
and his trip to blow the dust off a few neglected maps in
Africa. But insistent desire and his family's resources ap-
parently won the day.

After seeing the maps and talking with Lou Barnett and
Howard Walsh, Dick Moncrief approached his grandfather
about the possibility of making a deal to drill in Israel. It
was then that he was turned down by the older man with
such resounding sureness. The rebuff occurred, however, at
the same time that Bill Houck left Champlin Oil and came
to work for Dick Moncrief. Their alliance gave the younger
man the support he needed in order to challenge his grandfather and venture onto a wild new frontier.

Bill Houck was dispatched to Israel during the fall of
1974, upon his return from Djakarta. He arrived in Tel Aviv
at 4:45 in the morning, as he recalls it, with only the name
of David Sofer in his pocket; when he telephoned him from
the airport, Sofer said he knew nothing of the oil business,
hung up, and went back to sleep. Bill Houck was on his
own. He stayed around for a few days, and studied the oil
tax laws of Israel and its geology, and what he learned intrigued him.

He discovered that such information as he needed was
freely available. Bribery, at least in regard to the acquisition
of oil concessions, appeared to be little practiced in this
country, in contrast to what Bill Houck had seen during his
years of negotiating around the globe. He discovered also
that Israel's own geology was not good, and that the tax
structure would have made drilling within the country's
own borders an impossibility in any case. The occupied
lands along the northern arc of the Sinai desert were what
interested him. The Egyptians had made a rich discovery
near the Sinai Bedouin settlement of Abu Rodeis just before
they lost the land to Israel, and it was here that the trunkload of geology that Lou Barnett had brought to Fort
Worth indicated that oil might lie.

After returning to Fort Worth, Bill Houck paid a quiet visit to Panama City, to incorporate a company there that could buy rights to drill in the Sinai. "We went Panamanian," he said, "because it was easy. In Panama, there are all these companies with incorporation forms all written out, just waiting on a shelf for someone to fill in the blanks and sign them." Incorporation in Panama also offered tax advantages, and permitted Dick Moncrief and the Texans he brought in with him to retain their anonymity, a necessary consideration during an era of Palestinian sabotage.

Dick Moncrief and Bill Houck became officers of a new Panamanian company, Western Desert. Dick Moncrief gave shares in the venture to three of his Fort Worth friends—Howard Walsh, Lou Barnett, and Kelly Young. Western Desert then began negotiating to buy concessions to the Sinai desert. Sometimes the entire Fort Worth contingent went along to Israel for the ride.

They shuttled to New York on the Moncrief family's DC-9-sized BAC-111, with the gold-plated faucets and leather banquettes and champagne bar. They flew commercial from there, because taking the big plane overseas made Monty Moncrief nervous back in Fort Worth. They enjoyed traveling in a pack, as Texans so often do, and sometimes they brought their wives along. "We'd take the girls, and really put on the dog," Dick Moncrief recalls. "We knocked them out with our flash. But Israelis are like Texans, they understand it when you stick with your family. And they like you to give them a show."

The Texas contingent met with Zvi Dinstein, the Israeli government oil advisor, in the suite that Lou Barnett maintained at the King David Hotel in Jerusalem. This was during the winter and spring of 1974, when Henry Kissinger was also a frequent visitor at the King David, practicing what was becoming known as his "shuttle diplomacy" between the Israeli capital and Cairo. And although Bill Houck and Dick Moncrief kept their distance from Kissinger, his bargaining

paralleled and shaped the course of theirs. For he was negotiating Israel's withdrawal from the very lands whose mineral rights the Israelis were just then engaged in signing over
to Western Desert.

Time was of the essence in Western Desert's figuring. If
the Sinai were returned to Egypt before Dick Moncrief
found oil there, he would lose his deal completely. Thus
the heat of Kissinger's efforts to bring a quick peace worked
against him and Bill Houck during the season they spent at
the King David Hotel. Their own bargaining with the Israelis proved slow. Dick Moncrief was learning that end-
less haggling over detail was the very essence of Middle
Eastern trading technique.

But he wanted nothing less than a bargain he could call
"the greatest deal in the world," and he was willing to
spend time and many millions going after it. "I never cared
if I didn't make any money on this thing," he said once,
back home in Fort Worth. He stared at the map of the
world that stretched out across his office wall. It suggested
limitless frontiers, but when he turned to gaze out his window he saw only the highway ramp that circumscribed the
limits of his hometown. "I don't want to lose money, you
understand. But I don't care about making it. I just want
them all to know that I made the greatest deal in the world.
And I did. You can tell my granddad that."

Making the greatest deal in the world meant that Dick
Moncrief had to finance wildcat wells in the Sinai until he
made a discovery. Only then would the Israeli government
give him help and finance the development of his fields,
drilling the surrounding wells and pumping the formations
clean. He wanted the government to guarantee him development money, and he made their participation a stipula-
tion to his agreement. All through the winter of 1974, he
held firm on his demands.

He had to. He knew that no bank in America or anywhere
else in the world would finance the development of disputed

lands, and he knew that he himself could never raise the hundreds of millions needed to develop Sinai fields once oil was found. "Hell, it would have cost me more than a hundred million just to lay one pipeline," he said. Major companies usually develop big fields when independents find them in America, but no major was willing to step onto occupied Israeli soil. Dick Moncrief had no choice but to turn to the Israelis themselves.

They had no choice either. If they wanted Dick Moncrief, they had to promise him development money. And they must have wanted him, for during the course of negotiations, they sent a delegation from the government-backed Israel Discount Bank to look over the Moncriefs in Fort Worth. "That was really something, those Jewish bankers coming down to the old Fort Worth Club," Dick Moncrief recalled, relishing the picture of himself marshaling a parade of Orthodox visitors through the club rooms, heavy with the gilt and leather that signified a turn-of-the-century cattleman's idea of splendor. "But as I say, Israelis are like Texans. Everyone knows everyone else, and they do their business in a personal way. It didn't take them long to figure out what kind of man Granddad was, and once they understood our reputation, the deal was ours."

The Israelis granted Western Desert an exclusive concession to the northeastern Sinai lands, even though concessions, with their echo of an earlier imperialist era, were rarely given anymore; production sharing contracts had long since become the accepted form of agreement. The concession gave Western Desert full title to all the oil the company produced. The state of Israel, as landowner, received a royalty fee and tax revenues, but had to buy its own petroleum from the Texans.

The deal Dick Moncrief and Bill Houck made for themselves was a good one, but the earth proved stubborn and did not conform to the plans that men had made. The first well, drilled in the late spring of 1976, came in dry. "I just knew it wasn't going to come in," Dick Moncrief says. "We've been oilmen for three generations in our family, and we've got a sense of these things. I could feel it all in my gut, so I got out of Israel fast, and came home to wait for the bad news."

The first dry wildcat cost three million dollars. The next three wells cost eleven million, and they too came in dry. Looking at the wreckage around him in the desert, Dick Moncrief began to figure that he might have done something wrong this time, might have sacrificed prudence in the interest of being able to boast of the deal he had made. Things could continue this way, he knew, dry well following upon dry well, as he paid the full price for each and watched his millions melt away. He would be left with nothing to show for his efforts.

Already he had begun to hear rumors from the men who worked for him about bigger and richer strikes that might be made further south in the Sinai, down along the Gulf of Suez. Such rumors, however, could avail him nothing so long as he was limited by having his own mere millions to work with, for those millions were disappearing fast. To solve his problems, and to save his deal, Dick Moncrief knew that he had to find himself a partner. He needed someone who could command more money than he ever could, someone unafraid to risk it all in a land that the Arabs had declared off-limits to the entire world.

19

Code Name: The Project

AFTER WINNING CONTROL of the Sinai during the Six-Day War, Israel's National Oil Company (INOC) had assumed operation of the northern Abu Rodeis field, which Egypt had developed before it lost the land. The Israelis had also sponsored a number of exploration programs in the northern arc of the peninsula, but no immediate attempts to find oil had been made in the long stretch of desert to the south, or beneath the Gulf which lapped its shore. Egyptian gunboats patrolled these waters, and soldiers stood garrisoned along the opposite bank. Israel was reluctant to drill beneath the direct gaze of what was then her fiercest enemy.

When Kissinger's first disengagement treaty went into effect in 1975, however, the Abu Rodeis field was returned to the Egyptians. Israel lost her only sure supply of petroleum, and INOC, originally formed to search for oil in Africa, lost its reason for being. The men who headed that company began casting about to find another project.

What they came up with was "the Project," an operation so secret that even the Knesset, Israel's parliament, knew nothing of it. The Project was headed by Dr. Michael Keesh, an Israeli bureaucrat who had headed the Netevei Neft, the government company that managed Abu Rodeis. As was only natural, the Project employed many who had worked for the earlier company. Few of them had any experience exploring for oil. And yet the Project was formed for the purpose of wildcatting in perhaps the most difficult place in the world at the time—offshore, in the Gulf of Suez.

Keesh's first need was for a rig, so that the Project could commence drilling. Because of the Arab's boycott of companies that did business with Israel, oil-field equipment was almost impossible to come by. What contractor would risk billions of dollars worth of Arab business in order to sell a rig or two to Israel? Keesh had to use a Dutch cover to haul a shipwrecked rig—Rig Number Five—from Oman to Singapore, and then purportedly to Malta. It disappeared mysteriously, of course, along the Suez coast, where Keesh's forces stood ready to seize it.

Rig Number Five was old and rickety despite its overhaul, and drilling in the Suez would have proceeded with difficulty even if Keesh's minions had been more experienced. As it was, they chose their drill sites poorly, and all their efforts yielded only sixty barrels of oil, extracted at great cost. Dinstein, Israel's oil advisor and an enthusiastic champion of the Texans then operating in the north Sinai, proclaimed before his ministry that Israel's bureaucracy was not professional enough to drill in such treacherous waters. The assertion offended Dr. Keesh and lead to a rift between him and the ministry. When it became public, it blew the cover of secrecy that had protected the Project like a slick mantle of oil.

It was during this time that Dr. Tom Brown, a Texas geologist working for Moncrief International in Tel Aviv, first heard rumors that oil was being explored for in the south. He conveyed what he knew to Dick Moncrief and Bill Houck, who approached the government about buying concessions to drill in the Gulf themselves. They were met with silence. The southern Sinai and its waters were off-limits, they were told. But their efforts in the northern Sinai impressed the oil ministry, and as the rift with Dr. Keesh grew worse, the government offered to "go fifty-fifty" with the Moncriefs. The Israelis would split the costs of exploration in the Suez with Western Desert, and guarantee money to develop whatever fields were found.

Dr. Keesh, upon learning that his private, already crumbling fiefdom was about to be handed over to a couple of rich Americans, was outraged. He went on Israeli television to warn that the national treasure was being stolen by foreigners. Finally, he stormed before the Knesset and complained directly to the Prime Minister, who responded by asking for his resignation. The Project became a public scandal within the land of Israel, although the outside world would take little notice of it until two more years had passed.

After the government's offer to Dick Moncrief, Bill Houck and Tom Brown journeyed down to the Gulf port city of At-Tūr. They wanted to look at the possibilities for drilling offshore from that Bedouin village. They studied the geological mappings available, especially those that indicated a continuum of sands running through from the Egyptian side of the Gulf. The prospects looked good, but this only increased Dick Moncrief's problems, and convinced him even more that he needed a partner. He would have to find someone doubly rich and powerful if he wanted to take a chance on this newer, bigger, wilder gamble.

The Israeli government offered Dick Moncrief a 50 percent option to drill three wells in the south, wells mapped out by geologists who had worked under Keesh. After these were completed, they could go partners on wildcatting in the Gulf of Suez. Dick Moncrief took the option although he hadn't yet found the money to see him through. The first well, the RGM Number Two, was begun, but the ancient

Rig Number Five proved unequal to the task of drilling it. "The promised land was getting away from us," said Bill Houck, and indeed, throughout most of 1976, it looked as if the promised land might just be one more desert mirage.

Dick Moncrief and Bill Houck spent most of that year back in Texas, looking for a partner. Forty companies turned them down. They almost made a deal with a Canadian trucking magnate, then on his deathbed and eager for one great final adventure. But ten months of negotiations came to naught in September of 1976. By then, Israel was making plans to drill the second Suez well, for the RGM Number Two had proven dry as a bone. Drilling would commence on November 15, which gave Dick Moncrief six weeks in which to find himself a partner. If he couldn't, he would lose his option, and the millions he had poured into Israeli soil would be as good as thrown away.

"We were desperate," Bill Houck said later. "We couldn't imagine who would want to take a chance on alienating the Arabs by coming in with us on Israel. Finally Dick said, since we can't find what we want, let's make a list of what we need."

What they needed, besides big, big money, was a company that had a single man running it; no committees, no group decisions, no hierarchy of managers, no professional deal-killers or pessimists, no long waits for approval while the deal went down the drain, no stockholders eager to put in their two cents or Monday-morning quarterback a risky decision that failed. What they needed was a company that could play with hundreds of millions and was willing to gamble. The only place they knew of that sounded like that was the Superior Oil Company down in Houston, then the highest-priced public stock listed on the New York Exchange.

Superior, however, had dealings with the Arabs. Moreover, one of its subsidiaries held leases in Egypt. For that reason, Dick Moncrief hadn't even considered approaching

the company about partnership in Israel. But by September
of 1976, he was willing to try anything. "We decided what
the hell," said Bill Houck. "So we flew on down to Houston
and gave them our dog and pony show. A few days later
they called back and said they were interested, come on and
talk. It was unbelievable."

Unbelievable it might have been, but it was also true.
Within a few weeks, Superior had agreed to back Western
Desert in its Gulf of Suez venture. The hitch that necessi-
tated a last minute frenzy of negotiating, of wheeling and
dealing, of Bill Houck flying back and forth between Jerusalem, At-Tūr, Houston, and Fort Worth, came as a result of
Superior's refusal to go fifty-fifty with the Israelis and accept
INOC as its partner. Superior was willing to back Dick
Moncrief completely, to assume all the costs of exploration,
but the company wanted 100 percent control. It wanted a
full production-sharing contract that would permit it to produce all the oil and take 25 percent of it as payment.

"I was left to talk the Israelis into that one," Bill Houck
recalled. And he did so, although the terms of his agreement
were such that the Israeli press denounced the "giveaway"
as a national disaster, overlooking the fact that the government had never been able to find or produce any oil on its
own.

Superior did not openly assume title to the Sinai desert or
the Gulf of Suez. Nor did the company send someone in to
usurp Dick Moncrief's role as the man who made things
happen. Superior kept its profile low. Not until the following
year did the thick, slick, ivory-bound report sent out to
every stockholder take rather off-handed notice that a Superior subsidiary named Neptune had acquired an option to
buy the Western Desert Company that was then operating
abroad.

Neptune itself, chartered quietly in Panama just as Western Desert had been, moved behind the scenes of the Israeli
Deal like some shady giant from the sea. Israeli news ac-

counts railed against Neptune upon occasion, but nobody ever disclosed exactly what Neptune might be. The company of course was simply a device that enabled Superior to finance Western Desert. Neptune poured its hundreds of millions into Western Desert's drilling projects, explored the two Suez locations already mapped out by the old Project, and then went on and broke open the new frontier.

20

The Cadillac
of the Oil Business

THE SUPERIOR OIL COMPANY, through its subsidiary Neptune, took risks that other companies might have laughed at. They were risks that even Dick Moncrief, bringing his "dog and pony show" to Houston when he pitched his deal, had never dreamed the company would go for. And yet Superior's almost unaccountable decision was undertaken in the same spirit that had moved Dick Moncrief to search out the wildest, riskiest scheme he could find. Once again, it was the story of the old bulls and the young bulls and their fight to inherit the earth.

In 1976, the Superior Oil Company was a giant octopus of an entity, operating in sleekly entowered corporate splendor from the very center of power in Houston, the First National City Bank building. The company had six hundred million dollars at its disposal for oil exploration that year and was looking to spend every cent of it. The company was in the big leagues, was the biggest on the big board, but Superior was not in fact run as one might expect a large and far-reaching corporation to be run.

The company operated instead against the same rich, tenebrous background of family rivalry and the will to succession that gives color to many a private drama in Texas. Howard Keck, the president and undisputed ruler of Superior at the time, lived under the long shadow that had been cast over Houston by his father, a giant of the first generation. And it was in an attempt to vanquish that shadow and carve out a place for himself in the world that Howard Keck found himself willing to take a frontier gambler's risk with more than a hundred million dollars.

Howard Keck was the second son of an oilman from California named William Keck, who started Superior after he made one of the biggest strikes of the 1920s, in California's Kettleman hills. William Keck then became one of the first oilmen to move his business to Houston, which at the time was not much more an inadequately drained malarial swamp. The reality of Houston was dismal in the days before air-conditioning made 110 degree temperatures and 100 percent humidity bearable. But the reality was absurd as well, since Houston rested its claims upon being a port city when it was in fact fifty miles inland from the Gulf of Mexico. But reality has never deterred a frontier booster's spirit, and Houston was a booster's town. It was the kind of city that a determined optimist like William Keck could discern had a future, a future that could be made real.

William Keck was known throughout the company he had created as "the Old Man," and people called him that until the day he died. His character was strong and some said it was mean. His political views were fiercely conservative, but he was nimble and innovative when it came to doing business. He was the first independent to drill offshore in the Gulf of Mexico, and year after year he set records for the deepest-drilled well. He gambled on a big scale and earned Superior the epithet it still carries today, that of being "the

Cadillac of the oil business," the company with the cleanest
rigs, the sharpest engineers, and the highest salaries. Superior's field superintendents were known to drive Pontiacs
when everyone else was driving Fords.

William Keck ran his company like a one-man machine,
and he retained control of the stock even after it went public. He bequeathed it all to his sons of course, and there followed the double twist that adds its characteristic salt to so
many Texas dramas of succession. For the knife edge of old
bull competitiveness in this part of the world cuts so deeply
that it often cuts uncleanly, and fratricidal fallout is frequently the inevitable consequence.

The oldest of the Old Man's two sons was William Keck,
Jr. He succeeded naturally to the presidency of Superior,
but his younger brother Howard chafed under his rule. At
last he amassed power and support among Superior's employees, and when his position was solid he attempted a
coup. "The in-fighting was rough during those years," a sur-
vivor of the old regime recalled. "You had to watch that you
didn't get caught in the cross fire." A bitter battle ended in
defeat for the older son, who resigned as president, left the
company entirely, and then returned a decade later to the
ignominy of holding one seat among many on the board of
directors. Howard Keck, having won this nearly taboo struggle for absolute control, would not prove in later years to be
a man who shrank from the prospect of risk.

After taking control of Superior from his brother, Howard
Keck, a personally retiring, physically unprepossessing, be-
hind-the-scenes kind of man, sought ways to leave his own
mark upon the company his father had founded. He wanted
to carve his own tracings, leave his own legend behind in
Houston, a city where legends are writ large. His efforts did
not meet with unqualified success.

Immediately after his father's death in 1964, he began to
invest Superior's rich assets in silver and nickel and copper
mines. He bought agricultural lands in California to which

the company had formerly held only the mineral rights, hoping to profit from the bounties of the earth rather than seeking only what lay below. But Howard Keck knew little about minerals or farming. His expertise was in oil, and when he tried the second generation tactic of diversifying, Superior went into a decline. Its commodities ventures strayed into the red, and its reserves of oil in the ground fell by 67 percent.

The decline continued until the OPEC summit meeting in 1973, after which the oil business started heating up again. It was then that Howard Keck brought his business back into the fields with a vengeance, casting aside his program of diversification, hiring and firing geologists and petroleum engineers, and leasing up thousands of acres of land. By September of 1976, when Dick Moncrief and Bill Houck came to town with their deal, Superior's profits from oil and gas discoveries had increased fourfold in a few years.

But it was not Howard Keck that Dick Moncrief and Bill Houck visited in their last desperate weeks of looking for a partner. It was instead one of the men whom Howard Keck had enticed away from a major oil company when he decided to get his oil business back in shape. He had brought so many men into his company so fast that he'd caused a storm among the majors in Houston. Mobil Oil finally sued him for impairing the company's ability to do business.

Men left the majors and went to work for Howard Keck for the same reason that the geologist George Bouline had quit his comfortable job and come to chase the Golden Circle reef through Louisiana for Monty Moncrief. The same reason indeed had inspired Bill Houck, with a string of international jobs behind him, to settle in Fort Worth and go to work for a young man who had yet to make a successful deal abroad. These were men who wanted to take a risk, who wanted to share in whatever profits or losses their talents might bring. They were men who wanted, as Monty Moncrief had, to *better themselves,* and who measured that betterment by freedom and by money. Once the independents were back in business, there was no holding big talent among the majors. The best men went to work for themselves, or for companies not bound by the tight cautious ways of corporate structure.

Among these men was Joe Reid. He managed Superior's international operations at the time that Dick Moncrief and Bill Houck came to Houston to make their pitch on the Israeli Deal, and he acted as their advocate in the company and smoothed the deal. "I first met Dickie playing golf at some tournament over in Midland," he said later. "We used to holler back and forth whenever he came to town, but we never did any business together. I thought about it, but nothing ever happened until the day he turned up here with this Gulf of Suez thing."

Dick Moncrief showed his geology to Joe Reid, showed him how a seven-mile wide strip of rich Nubian production lay on the mirror side of the Gulf in Egyptian land. And although Joe Reid figured the deal had probably been shopped around all over Texas, he also understood that it had been rejected because of the political complications it presented, not because it didn't look like a good drilling bet. "I figured, what the hell, the situation everywhere in the world is unstable," he said. "There's no guarantee anymore, so maybe it's smarter to take a good geological deal and just let the politics take care of themselves."

Joe Reid's enthusiasm may have been stirred by his own infatuation with the entrepreneurial ideal. For although he has always been a management executive, a team player, a smooth company man, Joe Reid likes the idea of playing it fast and loose. He likes to speculate upon the "factors" that have made Monty Moncrief, for example, a great independent. He isolates these factors, breaks them down, parses and defines them, and compares his own opportunities for the application of frontier virtue to those that presented themselves to the older man, as if he were seeking to model himself upon a more heroic scale. Of course, it is impossible to imagine Monty Moncrief thinking in terms of such abstractions, or speaking (as Joe Reid speaks) of "the decision-making process." But then abstractions are important to Joe Reid, who believes it is possible to inject entrepreneurial skills into big business once the correct scientific system has been worked out. The Israeli Deal appealed to him because it offered an opportunity to make daring, risky decisions such as a real entrepreneur might make.

Despite his penchant for the jargon of modern management, Joe Reid's manner is no more that of the modern bureaucrat than that of any wildcatter. He was in his middle forties when Dick Moncrief came to see him, but he seemed much younger than that. He was insouciant and enthusiastic, and with his red hair and freckles and the thick rural-South accent he had kept all through Harvard Business School, he still appeared to be very much the backwoods Mississippi hayseed. He was naïve enough to endorse the philosophy of "I'm Okay, You're Okay" throughout lunch with a stranger, and to admit his awe of Dick Moncrief's natural ability to command the best table in any crowded restaurant he walked into. And he was loose enough to enjoy himself after work cruising along Houston's freeways, playing *Saturday Night Fever* tapes and singing along. He liked to stop off at an exit-ramp Holiday Inn for a couple of scotches sometimes, and would continue to do so after he was named the president of Superior. His pleasures were far from pretentious.

Joe Reid had been scouted by college football teams across the South, and had played at Louisiana State before a brief turn with the Los Angeles Rams. Afterward, he joined the Trunkline Oil Company in Louisiana, and his attitude remained that of the intelligent professional athlete, much concerned with technique and group decision. Joe Reid had played center, and so he was accustomed to pitching off to the quarterback instead of carrying the ball himself. He still pitches off to the quarterback at the Superior, and he likes the company because it subscribes to a strong quarterback theory of business. "Keck doesn't have to worry about taking heat from a tableful of second-guessers," he explains. "He took one look at the Israeli Deal and said, 'Take it, boys.' The truth is, we had to spend twenty million dollars just to find out that our first location was wrong. But hell, we could have thrown that away just buying leases."

Because Superior is a strong quarterback team, the Israeli Deal took only a few weeks to put together, and Dick Moncrief was able to meet his November first deadline for participating in the second Gulf of Suez well. Once the Israelis had been persuaded to grant the Texans full rights to the Gulf instead of a partnership, the deal between the Moncriefs and Superior could be cut and laid out during the course of a single Sunday afternoon.

A triple suite at the chill and cavernous Hyatt Regency Hotel in Houston was rented for the occasion. The Moncrief forces ensconced themselves on one side, while Joe Reid and his men were installed on the other. Neutral territory between them was set aside for bargaining. Dick Moncrief, grown weary of Middle Eastern styles of haggling, was happy to be back on home ground. He felt confident that each card would be played as it was laid, instead of being taken back for the renegotiation of points that had already been settled.

The primary point of contention between the two parties, the cutting edge of the deal, was the size of Western Desert's share in the venture Neptune had agreed to back completely. And just to make sure that things went to his family's satisfaction, Monty Moncrief had boarded his jet at the last minute and flown down to Houston. However thoroughly the old bull disapproved of the whole foreign scheme, as he called it, and however completely he had cut his grandson loose in his dealings abroad, Monty Moncrief's pride was nevertheless tied to his image of himself as a dealmaker. It was hard to stay away when a deal like this one was going down.

Perhaps there was also a subtle strategy in his coming to Houston. For although he did not participate, did not even enter neutral negotiating territory, the simple fact of his presence dominated the scene, as it always did. After all, hadn't his grandson Charlie spoken of how his grandfather liked to fly in at the last minute and announce that W. A. Moncrief was there, just to shake things up? After eighty-four years on earth, the old bull understood his own power, and he knew when to use it.

Throughout the course of that Sunday afternoon, Monty Moncrief sat in his family's suite, drinking Bourbon and watching the Dallas Cowboys game on television. He grumbled occasionally about the expense of renting out such lavish quarters, for the Gregg Hotel in Longview had been good enough for him, and he didn't go in for fripperies, as he called them. He kept relay teams of negotiators informed of what appeared for all the world to be uppermost in his mind that day—Dallas's score. The relays in turn kept Monty Moncrief informed about what was happening at the big table. When at last they emerged from their labors, Neptune had agreed to put up all the money required to drill the Gulf of Suez leases, and cut Western Desert in for a full 15 percent.

The bargain was struck easily that afternoon, between two groups of men eager to make a deal. And so it was that Dick Moncrief and Howard Keck, through his good-humored proxy Joe Reid, divided things up and agreed to go ahead with making the greatest deal in the world. In doing so, they sought to surpass the legendary deeds of older and tougher men, one of whom had come that day to be among them, and ensure that the birthright he had passed on was not squandered or bartered lightly away.

21

Baptism by Fire

NEPTUNE'S ENTRY into the Gulf of Suez made all the difference. The Israelis had been poor-boying it, making do with second-rate equipment, squeezing too many people into choppers too old and too small, and scrimping on electric logs. When Superior turned on the cash, everything changed.

The two locations mapped out by the old Project proved, upon drilling, to be dry. But then seismographs were taken, and careful new maps drawn up of the rock conformations that underlay the waves. "The Egyptians sort of sat there across the Gulf while we took our soundings," a Superior engineer recalled. "Every once in a while, they'd cruise in close, but Israeli gunboats would chase them off." The soundings revealed a long, flat plateau between two high rolls of reef along the Gulf floor. The rolls were rich accumulations of hydrocarbon-breathing fossils, and Dick Moncrief's geologist decided that oil must lie between them.

The plateau constituted what would become known as the Alma field, named (as was every well or field in this deal) after one of the negotiator's daughters. The first well there, the Alma Number One, took months to drill, and came in dry as a bone. "But we knew we had a site," said Dick Moncrief. "Tom Brown isn't wrong about these things, and my intuition told me this was it. We just needed to move over a few leagues and try again."

The second well, the Alma Number Two, came in so rich and deep that the testing equipment inherited from the old Netevei Neft could not even gauge its measure. It came in one year to the month after Neptune entered the deal, in November 1977. And of course, it came in on the very night before President Anwar Sadat of Egypt made his first visit to Jerusalem to negotiate for the return of the Sinai lands.

During Sadat's visit, only Israel's Prime Minister Menachem Begin, the National Oil Company President Israel Lior, and oil advisor Zvi Dinstein knew of the Alma discovery. Bill Houck had called Dinstein the night the well came in and begun negotiating for the forty-eight million dollars that the Israelis had promised them to begin developing the field. The next day, he had log readings flown to Jerusalem so that the ministers could see what the field looked like. Bill Houck and Dick Moncrief wanted the development money as soon as they could get it, for a sixty-day delay would mean sixty fewer days to pump oil before the field was lost to them forever. And with Sadat's sudden visit, it looked as if they might lose it all sooner than they had planned.

Although Bill Houck still spoke of "our fields" and "our development," a division of labors did in fact take place when Superior entered the Israeli Deal. Neptune assumed the exploration and production of the Suez, using old Western Desert people like the geologist Tom Brown. Dick Moncrief and Bill Houck turned their efforts toward trying to save their field from the threat of loss through political circumstance. Dick Moncrief had never learned to wheel and deal on these levels, and he had to learn the arts of international intrigue and leverage as he went along. His was to be a true baptism by fire.

The Texans had first of all to convince the Israelis that the discovery at Alma was important. Alma must be recognized, they said, as Israel's ace in the hole, a card not to be dealt away lightly. Next, they had to persuade the Egyptians to allow them to continue as operators of the field after the occupied lands had been returned. "We asked the Egyptians why they should bring in another oil company to screw around and waste time when we could be making millions every day for them right away," said Dick Moncrief. He further argued that the oil produced in the Suez should be sold to Israel by Egypt when the field was returned. And would not an independent financial mercenary like himself, without loyalty to either side, be the perfect conduit to act between these ancient enemies? "A good deal is a good deal for all," he liked to say, and the old wildcatter's adage seemed to apply in this case.

Of course there were problems with this argument. Among them was the inescapable fact that the Israelis had recently machine-gunned the buoys out of an Amoco drill ship attempting to drop anchor in the Suez, an act the Egyptians regarded as proof of enmity. And of course Bill Houck and Dick Moncrief had to persuade those who mattered in Washington that they had the right to be involved in Middle East peace negotiations in the first place. They felt that this particular pitch was the least successful, the least likely of getting them what they wanted. "The State Department always regarded us as intruders, people who just caused them a lot of trouble," Bill Houck explained.

He and Dick Moncrief decided they would have to work privately in Washington. They found little sympathy in Congress for their program, and were beginning to understand the truth of what Richard Nixon had once told Monty Moncrief, that "there just aren't enough of you boys to make any difference around here." They engaged a suite in the resplendent Madison Hotel, one floor from where the Israelis were ensconced and two floors from the Egyptians. They met with the ministries of both governments, and with the private agents who negotiated between them. Sometimes they persuaded the object of their attentions to board the big old BAC-111 or the more recently acquired de Havilland jet, and they would fly here and there while letting loose the full force of their argument. "Captive audience," Bill Houck explained. "In a plane, they can't escape."

Making their various pitches consumed the best energies of Dick Moncrief and Bill Houck during the two years that followed their first Suez discovery. The Israelis proved their most sympathetic listeners, for the significance of the Alma discovery became increasingly apparent as the size of the field there grew. After Alma Number Two came in, a whole series of deep-lying elephants were drilled. By the time Alma Number Three and Alma Number Four were in production, two million tons of oil a year were flowing, or forty thousand barrels a day, a full 25 percent of what Israel required. Twelve billion dollars worth of reserves were estimated to lie within its depths, reserves that were being drilled like hell, as Dick Moncrief said, gotten while the getting was good with a gusto that would have pleased the old frontier ghosts of Clint Murchison's East Texas Liberty Oil Company.

Pipes were set directly into Suez drilling platforms, and oil was pumped through them straight into the *Tratos*, a fifty-thousand-ton reserve tanker that stood at anchor five hundred meters from the field and served as a floating reservoir of oil. From there, thousands more tons flowed outward each day into a transport vessel called the *Apoikia*. Both ships were Greek, for that nation so monopolized the freighting and containment of oil around the globe that its companies could dare to do business with Americans in Israel without fearing Arab repercussions.

At just about this time, some "sweet little gas wells," as

Dick Moncrief called them, came in in the northern Sinai
fields to which Western Desert held exclusive concessions,
and that gas was also being lined into storage tanks inside
the state of Israel. New discoveries and increasing riches
continued to convince the Israelis that their discoveries
were important, and 1978 was proving the best of times in
regard to finding oil. But it was proving the worst of times
for political negotiating, and therein lay the rub.

Bill Houck came into the old Fort Worth Club where
Dick Moncrief was having lunch one afternoon in October
1978. He had come to announce that an entire fourth level
of pay rock had just been found at Alma Number Four. He
pulled from his topcoat a sheaf of electric logging charts
that had been taken over the wire from Tel Aviv that morning, and laid them on the table, tracing with his pen a delicate zigzag that indicated the new stratum of oil-saturate
sandstone.

"Now let's hear them talk about how old Monty's grandson is nothing but crazy," said Dick Moncrief, rubbing his
hands together over the charts, his natural high spirits getting the best of him as usual. "Even if we lose it all, they'll
have to say we went first class." But after the first few min-
utes of self-congratulation had passed, the old doubts returned. Things might look good here at home, but Washington had started to push for peace, a peace in which the
Israelis would lose their right to Sinai oil altogether. And it
looked as if Washington was about to salve over this loss by
guaranteeing Israel's entire oil supply for the next fifteen
years. Thus it was that two days after Bill Houck had ex-
ulted over new reports of well depth at Alma, Dick Moncrief announced that he had been beaten down.

He had not, of course. That very next year, in the autumn
of 1979, just as Israel was preparing to give Egypt back the
land it had won by war twelve years before, Dick Moncrief
was still in there fighting, flying to Egypt and trying to convince the foreign minister to keep him on in the Sinai. And

he was boasting, as he made ready to board the Concorde, that it was "the sexiest, most macho deal in the world," a contention that under the circumstances amounted to an attempt at self-description. No, Dick Moncrief was certainly not beaten down on Halloween night of 1978. "If there's anything this story's about," he told the visitor to whom he found himself telling the details of the deal he'd kept secret all over Texas, "it's tenacity." Being beaten down has nothing to do with tenacity.

And yet tenacity, even as thousands of barrels of oil were being pumped from the Alma field each day, was not enough to satisfy the challenge laid down that day on the Rivercrest golf course. Only success would do that, and success appeared doubtful, and a long time off. "We went first class on this deal," Dick Moncrief might say by way of consoling himself. But going first class didn't mean that much back home.

"Dickie still hasn't made any money on this deal," Monty Moncrief liked to remind people. "Let's remember that before we start talking about how exciting it all is." Glamour and international intrigue didn't count for much with the man whose legend had started it all. Cold cash was still the gauge by which he measured success or failure, and since it was on his turf that the challenge had been made, his were the rules that applied.

22

The Juice

"MONEY is just a tool for building ships," a Norwegian fleetowner, for a time thought the richest man in the world, once said. "It's not something I make so I can live like a king."

The shipowner's attitude is one that prevails among Texas oil independents, who reinvest 100 percent of their profits in new ventures, and who have never needed an incentive to plow their earnings back into the earth so long as drilling can yield the really big rewards when a well comes in.

In the high risk business of wildcatting, where one well in nine comes in, money is simply the chip one needs in order to stay in the game. Money—the fruit of the occasional big win—is also what one needs to prove that one has been blessed by the magic of luck, and thus is a worthy partner for anyone else who happens to want to play the game. Money is a tool in the oil business. Making it counts, not spending it.

"It's the money that makes you do it, don't forget that. Money is always the motivation," Dick Moncrief explained when asked about the tenacity that made him stick through the Israeli Deal. But in truth it was the idea of the money, not the money itself that mattered, the triumph of being able to say, *I did it, this is the measure of my achievement.* The money, beyond its use as a measuring stick for such claims, is itself incidental, for it can run so deep and rich in this business that there's no way of spending it all.

"Oh, you start daydreaming about ranches in Rio and that kind of stuff," Dick Moncrief said one afternoon, drinking an eighty-five-cent glass of white wine in a Fort Worth shopping mall restaurant. "But that's just gravy, just fixin's, just something to think about. Who really cares? There's only so much caviar you can eat."

And so once more, it's not the money. Dick Moncrief was born with as much of it as a man could want or use, and so were hundreds of other third-generation oilmen. And yet they've been going back into the fields since the frontier opened wide again, working like their self-made grandfathers once did.

Traveling through Texas oil country, it is easy to be blinded by the dazzle of wealth, blinded into overlooking the spirit of duty that lies behind its acquisition and so defines the Puritan spirit of this land. Spending money here is beside the point. Nor is money used as a means of ascending by slow movements some hierarchical social scale, as it might be in the East and almost always is in Europe. If you've got it here, you're already in. Money, in Texas, is not a means to the sweet life.

In Fort Worth, there are three museums, each of them distinguished enough for any large city to take pride in. They were built to house private collections, and to add to them. And stretching out west of town, there are homes that have been built as museums, by museum architects, to display private galleries of masterpieces that have made the journey from Paris or Rome to this flat, curious, lonely land. One sees these things, but one may not see that collecting art is regarded here as a worthwhile civic endeavor, a duty, almost like giving money to hospitals once was. Philanthropy of a more direct and human kind has become less personal as the government has attempted to take control of people's welfare.

In a tiny North Texas farm town like Spearman, where friendly "mother cows" pump oil all day and night from beneath the sorghum-planted high plains, there are whole developments of quarter-million-dollar houses, flung up suddenly on the edge of nowhere, and crowding the new-made streets are big Chevy vans and Cadillacs. There is a private airstrip (one among many) big enough to accommodate a large city. There is a general store from which lynx and chinchilla and ermine and every variety of mink may be ordered by catalog. One sees these things, but one may not notice that there are no restaurants in town except for the local Dairy Queen, still the favorite gathering place. One may not therefore see that life here, despite the luxury of its basic means of shelter, warmth, and transport, is as gritty and isolated as it was in any makeshift frontier shack.

Everywhere in Texas there are replicas of Houston's famous suburb River Oaks, stretching out to the north or west of town. In these suburbs, vast winding wooded tracts, millionaires old and new live in mansions built in every imaginable style—Colonial, Norman, Tudor, office-modern. Their thick lawns and elaborate borders of monkey grass and magnolia are tended in the heat by whole platoons of silent Mexicans, working all day long. Inside these homes (and there are thousands of them), where windows are sealed tight against the outside air and curtains drawn against the light of the sun, women prepare their elaborate toilette, dressing and undressing with special care simply to go to the bank or the cleaners. They consume their idle hours tending the finest blooms among their flowers, and they manufacture work for themselves by means of redecorating schemes and projects for charity or cultural improvement, intended to sweeten and soften life in their town. One sees this, but one does not always see that, although women are the spenders here, their elaborate homes and clothes providing a splendid show of wealth, their efforts really do not count for much. They are a superfluity that has nothing to do with the business of life, which of course is business, achievement, the mining and marking of the land.

Women may bring such touches of civilization to the plains as they can materially conceive; but was it not after all to escape that civilization that men came to the frontier in the first place? And is it not because they have always borne the role of civilizers that women here are both cherished and disregarded entirely? The spirit in this land is still a masculine one, and outside the cloistered, air-cooled homes, where it counts, money is not for spending; it is simply a tool for finding oil. All the Cessnas and de Havillands and Silverados and cream-colored Sevilles are merely modern workhorses, in the service of men who are out to get while the getting is good.

The second generation, having come of age in an era when the frontier appeared to be closing, was often seduced by the wealth that it had not earned and had no means of extending in a way that could challenge what had already been accomplished. The dilemma was expressed by an old Fort Worth lawyer, a man who had married one of Texas's great heiresses. After his marriage, he quit the practice of law and devoted himself to collecting legal memorabilia, antique seals and charters, and old prints of days in court. He watched his wealth grow as the estate lawyers diversified it, *spread it* like the Murchisons and Sid Richardson's heirs had done. "The problem is money," the lawyer said, one Bourbon-soaked afternoon, as he waved a vague hand at the walls of his office where treasures hung in gross profusion. "What's the use of practicing law when you can make more just sitting still? If you've got everything, you lose the juice. There's nothing to fight against anymore."

Nothing to fight against. And yet, if the third generation is different (*not content,* as Tom Marsh had said), it may be partly because the second generation left behind a legacy of uselessness and lack of achievement for them to fight against.

One hot March at midday, a Fort Worth heiress of the third generation received a visitor into her parents' home, a granite villa spread out like some great doge's palace, Venice on the open plains. Together, she and her visitor walked through paneled halls lined with trophies of the hunt. A corridor of moose heads, stuffed tortoises, and elephants' feet set on polished marble lead into a study that recalled those nineteenth-century private showcases which, like the Frick House or J. P. Morgan's Library, have long since become public showplaces in other parts of the country. The pelt of a tiger shot by a maharaja in some remote jungle lay atop a thick pile of assorted skins. Fabergé bronzes of Cossacks on horseback and blued steel revolvers inlaid with pearl crowded the gilt desk top. Everywhere the indiscriminate spoils of continents and of centuries lay jumbled together.

The heiress, who was married and lived down the road in a modest brick bungalow, sat at the desk in the library and made a few calls on a white plastic telephone crowded incongruously among the marble and bronze. Her visitor sat opposite in an opulent but monstrously uncomfortable leather chair, and remarked silently upon the wisdom of Henry James's observation that Americans, while they like the idea of luxury, are unable to distinguish a hard chair from a soft.

The phone calls were soon interrupted by a message from the heiress's mother. It seems she had a problem. Whenever she dressed for the evening, she could never remember exactly what jewelry she had, or which set went with what. She wanted her daughter to photograph everything she kept in the vault, set by set. She herself was busy, orchestrating cultural festivities for the next season in town.

A maid brought two paper grocery sacks downstairs to the heiress, and she and her visitor carried them outdoors, where they could be photographed in the sun. A ragged old velvet cape was spread upon the brown grass of early spring, and a succession of jewels was taken from moleskin-wrapped packages and laid upon it. The jewelry was divided by its settings. First came the diamonds set in gold, then the diamonds and pearls, then pearls alone, then amethysts, then coral set in silver, then rubies . . . Case after case was unwrapped, and the contents photographed with an Instamatic. When the film was being changed or more jewelry was being fetched, the visitor, unknown to anyone in the city of Fort Worth before that very afternoon, was left alone with the treasures, trusted without question for reasons that could not be guessed.

"Mother thinks an album of her jewels will help her get organized," the heiress explained, adding as an afterthought, "Can you imagine having all this junk? Being tied down by it? I'm glad I was born when I was, and don't have to live like this."

She shoved some coral and diamond pieces into the paper bag, and resumed her afternoon chore. She displayed as little self-consciousness as a daughter in another city might have shown watering the lawn while talking with a guest.

If the third generation is rebelling in part against the ostentation and love of display that trapped so many of their parents, whose inherited fortunes confused and paralyzed them and so consumed their energies, the third generation is also facing a frontier that, however temporarily, lies open once more before them in the oil business. The opening gives them the means to carve a place for themselves amid all that has gone before. It gives them what the Fort Worth lawyer, lost amid his collection of memorabilia, said he just didn't have and couldn't summon. *The juice*, something to fight against.

23

Better Luck This Time

"IT'S THE MONEY that makes you do it, don't forget that. Money is always the motivation." Dick Moncrief insisted on his point. But as he spoke, he outlined upon a piece of paper the details of the deal which, he had declared time after time, would probably never make him a cent. "I don't care if I never make a penny from this deal," he had also said, referring to Israel. "Just so long as I don't lose anything."

In the end, he didn't lose anything, although he didn't make anything either. At Haifa, in September of 1979, the greatest deal in the world fell apart.

For a long time, Dick Moncrief had thought that a trade agreement between Israel and Egypt might be the best guarantee of peace between the two countries. At Haifa, Egypt and Israel signed such an agreement. Israel would buy two million tons of oil each year from Egypt, roughly the amount then being produced in the Alma field; this would meet 25 percent of the nation's requirement. Another 25 percent would come from Mexico, while 50 percent would be bought from oil traders on the spot market. If the

Israelis were boycotted, the United States would buy oil on spot and resell it to them. The Haifa agreement solved Israel's oil importing problems, while giving substance to its treaty of peace with Egypt.

The agreement was well regarded around the world. But in Fort Worth it signaled the end of something, and that something was an optimism regarding an independent's chances for doing quick business abroad. For although Dick Moncrief's plan proved a success, he found himself dealt out of the game in the end. Egypt refused his pleas to keep him on as the producer of the oil he had found in their territory while it was occupied. And Israel declined to make his continued presence a condition of their signing any agreement. When Egypt took back the Gulf of Suez and the Sinai strip, Dick Moncrief lost all claim to the Alma field, and to the share of the riches he had discovered.

Such were the treacheries of international dealing, as Dick Moncrief had first learned when the government official with whom Bill Houck had just signed a contract in Angola suddenly disappeared, "back to the bush." Political maneuverability did not necessarily mean political strength when one was dealing with the intricacies of foreign government and alliance. The flexibility of a modern veal chop man availed him nothing when events overtook his plans.

Although Dick Moncrief lost the deal on which he had hoped to pin his reputation, he did not in the end lose his money. The price of oil rose so quickly that it protected him. During the year that passed between the discovery of the Alma field and the signing of the Haifa agreement, the price of oil on the international market went from twelve to eighteen to twenty-four to thirty dollars a barrel. It was a protection he never expected.

The Alma field also proved richer than anyone could have guessed, and continued to prove so with every several months that passed. By late 1979, the wells there were producing 40,000 barrels of oil a day. And because Dick Moncrief had, as he said, drilled like hell, lining his oil directly into the Greek transport tanker waiting offshore, he managed to recover the forty million dollars just a few weeks before the Suez and Sinai were returned to Egypt.

By his own measure then—"I don't care if I never make a penny from this deal—just so long as I don't lose anything," —Dick Moncrief's deal in Israel had been a success. It certainly established him as an international wheeler-dealer, a man with a wild and bold imagination. The very autumn that he was losing his field, financiers from Switzerland and the Middle East were flying to Fort Worth to court him, to romance him, as they say in Texas, with their diverse schemes. He had a reputation now, although he remained almost completely unknown to the public. His map of the world was stretched out across his office wall, and he had left his mark upon it, for however brief a time.

Yet the failure of the Israeli Deal by the standard oil business measure of how much money an investment yields made him question the compulsion that had driven him abroad. He had proven himself by this time, of course, and so had no reason to recall the peculiar fierceness of his desire for anonymity, his wish to establish himself independently from his family. It was that fierceness that had driven him once.

The arguments he had turned on his grandfather to make a case for an independent working abroad began to turn back on him. He had told his grandfather, for example, that the majors were no longer a competitive force abroad, because new laws had been passed that hindered public companies from bribing officials in other countries, and because their policy of long-range planning would discourage their investing in lands made unstable by political change and revolution. These things were true of course, but Dick Moncrief had failed to consider the political power the major companies wielded by virtue of their alliances in Washington, D.C.; nor had he considered the staying power that great corporations have. Amoco had simply waited him out in the Suez by keeping busy with other things during Israel's twelve-year occupation of the Sinai. Independents like himself could maneuver quickly, it was true, could get in and deal and get out again. But they also had to work quickly. They didn't have the money or resources to wait out the passing of war and peace.

Dick Moncrief had argued that *the world* was the new frontier, but now he began to consider that America was part of the world, even if his granddad had "done it all" in America. Central Africa still held his interest, as it did Bill Houck's, but his desire to do business there was tempered, in the days after Israel, by his awareness of the risk. Compulsion untempered by an awareness of the consequences means simple energy spun out to no purpose. The true gambler always knows the odds, and elects to play despite them.

After Israel, then, Dick Moncrief's interests turned to America, where his family's interests had always lain. It turned especially toward the Rocky Mountains, where the real romance in the oil business had gone; the frontier there was technological as well as geographical, for the oil in the great mountain chain lay within rocks that had been folded under, thrust up, and folded over again, and some of it had lost so much pressure that it had turned to tar. The sudden rise in the price of oil made it possible now to consider drilling these vast reserves, and for the first time Dick Moncrief began to think about doing so. He had about him the air of a man who had already made his point in life.

He was also interested in Mexico. During the very years of OPEC's ascendancy, discoveries had been made in that country along Texas's border that made it appear likely that it would yield as much power in the world in the 1980s as Saudi Arabia had during the 1970s.

The Texas-Mexico connection went back to the turn of the century, to the days when the Eagle Oil Company had drilled fifty salt domes in the Isthmus of Tehuantepec.

American holdings had been appropriated after the Mexican revolution, but wildcatters from Texas had kept a hand in things through private agreements. An itinerant family known collectively as the Brady Brothers had kept rigs in Mexico after nationalization, and they negotiated with Mexicans in the 1940s for the right to cut through the cedar and mahogany jungles of the south in their search for minerals. This venture, which the Bradys incorporated as the Pan American Sulfur Company, was backed by a group of wildcatters from the north who called themselves the Little Mothers of Dallas.

After the rich discoveries of the late 1970s, Texans began to strengthen the individual ties with Pemex, Mexico's national oil company, that had never been severed. Independents were disgusted with the U.S. government's seeming incapacity for building an alliance with Mexico and assuring favorable import agreements. Big dreamers began to see themselves as the potential link in the chain that would inevitably unite America's fortunes with those of Mexico, and they rushed forth to cultivate old connections. Dick Moncrief's best friends—men whom he'd brought in on the Israeli Deal—were among them, and he could not remain untouched by their fervor. The word was out: Mexico was the real new frontier.

As the 1980s began, Texans of the third generation were convinced that they were in the right place at the right time, just as their ancestors had been. They saw bureaucracy as narrowing possibilities throughout the rest of the country; they saw, for example, how the power wielded by the mining unions in the East was slowing the coal industry's reentry into the business of producing energy. Texas, they were quick to remind the visitor, was still only 13 percent unionized, and the closed shop was illegal in the state. Nor did businesses have to pay any state tax. The legislature in Austin met for a four-month session every two years, a policy adopted in an effort to dissuade the passing of new laws. Encouraging a capital economy was still the ideal in Texas, and those with ambition took what advantage of it they could, within the defined boundaries of good-old-boyism.

Because so many of the first generation in Texas established themselves as legends, carving their tracings deep across the land they were the first to settle, there has been for many years a feeling, a suspicion, that those who have chosen to follow in their wake can never meet their measure as men. If the old bulls are the longhorns in this drama of succession—lean, rangy, and fit for tough times, roaming the range and informing the spirit of the place like modern-day white buffalo—then it follows that the young bulls in the story may be the Herefords who came after them, tame creatures of fenced ranching, domesticated, meaty, and bland.

And yet as long as the open frontier remains, unbounded by precise geographical definition and expanding because of worldwide competition, the sight of the limitless horizon remains. And as long as it does, some of those who might have been Herefords will be inspired to walk in the paths of the longhorns who went before them.